AF660942

THE FAMILY AND THE NATION

Acharya Mahapragya

A.P.J. Abdul Kalam

The Family and the Nation

HarperCollins *Publishers* India

First published in India by
HarperCollins *Publishers* in 2008
HarperCollins *Publishers* India, Cyber City, Building 10-A, Gurugram,
Haryana – 122002, India

www.harpercollins.co.in

1 2 3 4 5 6 7 8 9 10

Copyright © Acharya Mahapragya and A.P.J. Abdul Kalam 2008

P-ISBN: 978-81-7223-747-9
E-ISBN: 978-93-5029-260-0

Acharya Mahapragya and A.P.J. Abdul Kalam assert the moral right to be identified as the authors of this book.

All rights reserved. No part of this publication may be reproduced, stored in a retrieval system, or transmitted, in any form or by any means, electronic, mechanical, photocopying, recording or otherwise, without the prior permission of the publishers.

Without limiting the exclusive rights of any author, contributor or the publisher of this publication, any unauthorized use of this publication to train generative artificial intelligence (AI) technologies is expressly prohibited. HarperCollins also exercise their rights under Article 4(3) of the Digital Single Market Directive 2019/790 and expressly reserve this publication from the text and data-mining exception.

Typeset in 10.5/14 Century Schoolbook
Jojy Philip New Delhi - 110015

Printed and bound at
Repro India Ltd.

*

HarperCollins *Publishers*, Macken House, 39/40 Mayor Street Upper, Dublin 1, D01 C9W8, Ireland

Contents

Acknowledgements

In writing this book, our ideas have been shaped by our interaction during the past few decades with millions of our countrymen hailing from different walks of life. Each interaction enhanced our experience and added to our understanding of the development of a noble family, a noble society and a noble nation. While embarking on this journey of writing a book, we realized the magnitude of connectivities involved and the extent of our society's evolution during the last few centuries. We realized too the extent to which it had been influenced by the people who had come to our country for various purposes. We particularly thank Dr Y.S. Rajan and all those people who have facilitated our understanding of our society and its unique characteristics.

Acharya Mahapragyaji would like to place on record his thanks to a number of devotees and followers who have contributed towards crystallizing his thoughts in this book. He particularly thanks Niyojikaji Sadhvi Vishrut Vibha, Prof. Muni Mahendra Kumar, Dr Sohanlal Gandhi and Prof. Arun K. Tiwari for their continuous involvement in the book and for enriching its content.

A.P.J. Abdul Kalam would like to thank the thousands of world citizens with whom he is virtually connected all the time and who provided him the inspiration for working towards the development of a value-based, prosperous, happy, peaceful and safe society keeping family as the foundation. He profoundly thanks Maj. Gen. R. Swaminathan for going through all the chapters and providing useful inputs for enriching the content. The book would not have taken this shape without the untiring and dedicated efforts of Shri R.K. Prasad and Shri Dhan Shyam Sharma in the preparation of the manuscript and its subsequent editing.

We also thank Shri Krishan Chopra, Shri Amit Agarwal and their team at HarperCollins for their excellent support.

Birth of the Book

Acharya Mahapragya is a fount of knowledge who purifies every soul that comes into contact with him. My first experience with him was at the Adhyatma Sadhna Kendra, Mehrauli, in October 1999. It was around midnight, and Acharyaji had prayed three times with his distinguished Jain monks for the welfare of the nation and the people. After the prayers, he turned to me and said words that still reverberate in my mind. He said, 'Kalam, God bless you for what you have done with your team. But the Almighty has a bigger mission for you and that is why you are here with me today. I know our country is a nuclear nation now. But your mission is greater than what you and your team have done; it is indeed greater than what any human being has ever done. Nuclear weapons are proliferating in tens and thousands in the world. I command you and you only with all the divine blessings at my disposal to evolve a system of peace wherein these very nuclear weapons will be ineffective, insignificant and politically inconsequential.'

When Acharyaji finished his message, a hush fell over the hall. It appeared to me as though the confluence of heavens concurred with the saintly message. For the first time in my life I felt shaken. Since then, Acharyaji's message has become my guiding light, and making it a reality a challenge that has given a new meaning to my life.

After that meeting, I met Acharya Mahapragya a number of times, and all my meetings with him gave me the distinct feeling that our conversations must have a higher purpose and that it must make itself manifest in some way. However, at that time, I did not know how that would happen. On 2 August 2005, I met Acharya Mahapragya again on the occasion of the conferment of the National Communal Harmony Award on him. We were seated together, and Acharayaji said, 'Kalam, the time has come to translate our thoughts into action—developing a peaceful, happy and prosperous society through the development of the family and the nation. And this we will do in the form of a book.' We thought over the question of how a noble nation could be formed and came to the conclusion that its seeds need to be sown in the family. Only an individual who has been brought up in a family that instils the right values will be able to realize his or her responsibility towards the nation. Such a citizen will adopt the principle 'work with integrity and succeed with integrity'. This premise is the bedrock of the book, which is why we have named it *The Family and the Nation*.

NOBLE NATION

A beautiful and yet distinct
Reddish light engulfed the galaxy,
The Milky Way, our galaxy.
All the stars were surprised with the alarm,
Wherefrom this lovely powerful light,
Who emanates, who emanates,
That was the cry of the galaxy.

I will answer, my friends:
'Oh my galaxy friends, I am the Sun,
I have eight planets in orbit,

One of them is Earth,
Carries six billion human lives.
They live in hundreds of nations.
One of the nations with great civilization,
India 2020, celebrates the birth of the noble nation.
Light of celebration from India reaching our galaxy,
Nation with clean environment without pollution,
Having prosperity without poverty,
Peace without fear of war,
The happiest place to live.'

—A.P.J. Abdul Kalam

Part 1

THE EVOLUTION

1

The Dynamics of Indian Culture

The human being is his own salvation,
and that is through three jewels:
Right Faith, Right Knowledge
and Right Conduct.

—Lord Mahavira

India is changing and a new nation is emerging before the eyes of the world so swiftly, so palpably that we can all watch the process. Out of this awakening is arising a new Indian renaissance, which will determine its future. There are, of course, many problems the nation faces today. To deal with these problems in the light of the Indian spirit and with a greater synthesis of science and spirituality is a difficult task but it must be undertaken.

Indian civilization has been the form and expression of a culture as great as any in human history—great in religion, philosophy and science, great in thought, great in literature, art and poetry, great in the organization of society and politics, great in craft and trade and commerce. Indeed, in what field has India not accomplished great things?

Indian culture has been enriched by extraordinary spiritual leaders, thinkers and saints. The values enshrined in the Vedas and the epics—the Ramayana, the Upanishads, the Mahabharata—created a deep impact on Indian literature and life. In Indian history, we see the convergence of many civilizations and cultures, which enriched India spiritually.

In mathematics, astronomy and chemistry, the chief ingredients of ancient science, Indians discovered and formulated much and anticipated, by reasoning or experiment, some of the scientific ideas and discoveries which Europe arrived at much later. India was well-equipped in surgery and her system of medicine survives to this day, though it declined intermediately in knowledge and is only now recovering its vitality.

Culture is a powerful human tool for survival, but it is also a very fragile phenomenon. It is constantly changing and is easily lost because it exists only in our minds. There are many layers of culture that are part of our enlightened behaviour patterns and perceptions. Most obviously it is the body of cultural traditions that distinguishes a specific society. When we speak of Indian culture, we are referring to the shared languages, traditions, and beliefs that set one group of people apart from others. In most cases, those who share a culture do so because they acquired it as part of their upbringing by parents and other family members. This chapter takes a long view of the evolution of Indian culture starting from the advent of human civilization.

TIIE INDIAN CULTURE

Indian society is multifaceted to an extent perhaps unknown in any other of the world's great civilizations. Virtually no generalization made about Indian society is valid for all of the nation's multifarious groups. Comprehending the complexities of India's social structure has challenged scholars and other observers over various periods of time.

The culture of India has been shaped by its long history, its unique geography, its absorption of customs, traditions and ideas from some of its neighbours, as well as by preserving its ancient heritage from the Indus Valley Civilization onward. India was repeatedly invaded across its land borders from Europe, West Asia and Central Asia and occupied in three waves for about 1325 years. Then the fourth wave arrived from across the seas with the British and other European powers, and lasted 227 years. This fusion of multiple cultures and civilizations is the unique character of Indian civilization. Living within the embrace of the Indian nation are vast numbers of different regional, social, and economic groups, each with different cultural practices. It is important to trace how Indian culture evolved.

As the people left their original forest dwellings to come to villages and towns, new social, economic and governmental systems developed, sowing the seeds of what came to be termed as a culture. Cities started becoming larger and more sophisticated, and people migrated out of villages and farms and flocked to the urban centres to take up various occupations which were no more dependent on Nature or handicraft but on fellow human beings and their interests.

According to Jain beliefs, Rishabh, born to King Nabhi Raja and Queen Marudevi at Ayodhya, in the Ikshvaku clan, existed before civilization developed. Scholars put the date of Rishabh at the end of the Stone Age and the beginning of the Agriculture Age. Terracotta seals and other evidences unearthed in the ancient cities of Harrapa and Mohenjo-daro provide a link between Rishabh and the Indus Valley Civilization. Rishabh taught people agriculture, tending of animals, cooking, and more. He had one hundred and one sons. His eldest son, Bharat, was the conqueror of the known world. According to Jain belief, India was named Bharata after him. The second son of Rishabh was Bahubali, whose statue stands at Shravanabelagola in Karnataka.

The human propensity for accumulation gave birth to conflicts among men. To resolve the conflicts the concept of community authority emerged. The head of the human community was called a Kulkar, who formulated the penal policy based on a verbal rebuke (hakaar neeti). As the instinct of possessiveness grew stronger and conflicts became more intense, the verbal rebuke was made harsher into censuring (makaar neeti) and later into outright damning (dhikkaar neeti).

Rishabh reorganized the population under his rule according to their virtues, activities and professions, and broadly divided society into three functional groups.

On the basis of occupation, four castes (jatis) were systematized, namely: (1) Ugra (security); (2) Bhoja (teacher); Rajnya (friends circle of Rishabh) and Kshatriya (the remaining classes). Rishabh had organized these castes as the chief of the community and not as a religious leader.

Philosophically, there are two important aspects of life: activity (pravritti) and abstinence from activity (nivritti). No society can survive without undertaking any activity or work. At the same time, no society sans abstinence can become rich in conduct or noble in character. The Vedic school of thought is characterized by the elements of activity, while the Shramanic tradition emphasized abstinence. It is by the amalgamation of both that Indian society remained dynamic as well as rich in morality and conduct.

The ancient Indian view of the individual and his relation to society is indeed based on an in-depth perception of a four-fold aim of human existence. The aims of human life have been summed up in a very well thought out pattern of aspiration designated as Dharma, Artha, Kama and Moksha. Anything that can be contacted through the sense organs, anything that can be possessed as property, and anything that is regarded as material value is Artha. Kama is the psychological value of human life. The human value, which at the same time surpasses itself, reaching beyond itself in a superhuman grasp of a cosmic principle, is Dharma. An intelligent investigation into the structure of this pattern, namely, the coming together of Artha, Dharma, and Kama, will reveal to us the profundity of this research and its final finding. The spiritual value of life, we may say, is what people generally think of as Moksha, a difficult term to properly understand in its linguistic form or even in its philosophical content. When the individual rises to the level of a spiritual aspiration, he ceases to be a limited individual social unit but becomes an embodiment of a call which is above all individual values or social relationships.

The concept of the values of life as Dharma, Artha, Kama and Moksha is a masterstroke of the genius of the Indian soil. It does not exclude from its consideration even the lowest aspects of human nature, but is also not satisfied with any of the aspirations of human nature. While all our desires are permissible in one way, none of the desires is finally permissible. While all that we need and call for, and every thought, every feeling, every vision of life is a permissible and valid evaluation of things from their own point of view, none of them is final. All angles of the vision of life are valid from their point of view—every religion is a right religion, a correct vision of things, every faith is valid in its own way, every vision is complete, every viewpoint has a validity of its own—anything that you think is valid thinking.

VISION OF SELF-RULE

In ancient times, India was known as the land of the Rose Apple (Jambu Dvipa). Both Buddha and Mahavira were born, and lived all their lives, in north-central India, in the area known as the Middle Land, so called because it was believed to be, by the people who lived there, the centre of the earth. The whole area consists of a vast fertile plain through which flow two great rivers, the Ganga and the Yamuna, and many small rivers. There are three seasons—summer, when the temperature can exceed the temperature of the human body; the rainy season, when the rivers flood and travel becomes difficult; and winter, when the days are pleasant but the nights can be freezingly cold. There was plenty of arable land for farming and most people had more than enough to eat. Even very poor farmers could supplement their diet or income by hunting wild animals and collecting the abundant fruits that the forests provided.

The India of those times was not a single political unit but rather a collection of independent countries that often vied with one another for supremacy. The civilized part of India was divided into sixteen realms, eight of which were kingdoms and the remaining republics. The largest and most powerful of these countries was the kingdom of Magadha, which during most of Mahavira's life was ruled by King Bimbisara, a strong and effective ruler who took great interest in religion. The capital of Magadha was Rajagriha (modern-day Rajgir, about 100 kilometres south of Patna), which nestled amongst rugged hills and was protected by massive stone walls, the remains of which can still be seen.

Directly north of Magadha and separated from it by the Ganga was the Vriji Confederacy. The Vriji Confederacy was made up of several tribes, two of which were called the Licchavi and the Videha, which had united to protect themselves from their powerful neighbour in the south. The Licchavi was the most important tribe in the Confederacy and their chief city, Vaishali, was the de facto capital of the Confederacy. It was in the Licchavi tribe that Mahavira was born as Vardhamana to King Siddhartha and Queen Trishala in 599 BC.

Four Jain Tirthankars[1]—Rishabh, Arishtanemi, Parshva, and Mahavira—undertook journeys into lands not inhabited by the Aryans. In 25 BC, King Pandya sent ambassadors to the court of Augustus Caesar. Innumerable Indian mendicants lived in West Asia, Egypt, Greece and Ethiopia.

Ancient India had a long history of government by discussion, in which groups of people having common interests make decisions through debate, consultation, and voting. Though evidence of non-monarchical government goes back to the Vedas, republican polities were most common and vigorous in the period of Mahavira. At this time, India was in the throes of urbanization. There was upheaval and struggle among the ordinary people.

The Pali Canon gives a picturesque description of the city of Vaishali in the fifth century BC as possessing 7707 storied buildings, 7707 pinnacled buildings, 7707 parks and lotus ponds, and a multitude of people, including the famous courtesan Ambapali, whose beauty and artistic achievements contributed mightily to the city's prosperity and reputation. The cities of Kapilavatthu and Kusavati were likewise full of traffic and noise. Moving between these cities were great trading caravans of 500 or 1000 carts. India was indeed a landscape with kings aplenty, a culture where the monarchical thinking was constantly battling with another vision of self-rule by members of a guild, a village, or an extended kin-group—in other words, any group of equals with a common set of interests. This vision of cooperative self-government often produced republicanism and even democracy comparable to classical Greek democracy.

INDIAN THOUGHT

Human beings, faced with the vastness of the Universe, could not but be filled with awe at the unfathomable immensity around them. Man was fascinated by the Universe, which seemed alien and eternally remote and at the same time conveyed to him a feeling that there was a unity to it and that he was an integral part of it. However far we go back in comparative religion, we find that this sense of the Universe as an integrated whole is common to all religions.

There were three kinds of disciplines: (1) pertaining to secular field (Laukika); (2) pertaining to Vedic culture (Vedic); and (3) pertaining to Shramana Culture (Samayika). The values of vows (Vrata) and self-restraint (Samyam) were the main contributions of the Shramana tradition. Mathematics, political science, penal code, commerce, arts, science, medical science (Ayurveda), sociology, economics, erotic science, psychology and similar areas related with worldly affairs were considered the Laukika disciplines. They had no relationship with any religion or philosophy. The *Sthananga Sutra* enumerates ten codes of righteous conduct (dharma): (1) concerning villages (gram dharma); (2) concerning cities (nagar dharma); (3) concerning nation (rashtra dharma); (4) ascetic orders of the Shraman culture (pashanda dharma); (5) concerning family (kula dharma); (6) religious group (gana dharma); (7) religious order (sangha dharma); (8) spiritual knowledge (shruta dharma); (9) ascetic practices (charita dharma); and (10) the cosmological substance, which is the medium of motion for all other substances (astikaya dharma).

The relationship that exists between society and economic resources can be compared to that of the body and the vital force (prana). Just as the body cannot survive without the vital force, a society cannot sustain itself without economic resources. We know little about the economic system that might have prevailed before the Vedic period. Cattle and agriculture were the main drivers of the economy along with mineral wealth. What is important to note is that ethical values were not neglected.

The post-Vedic period is marked by Kautilya's treatise on political economy (*Arthashastra*). There is a mention of unjust money (arthabhasa). According to the twelfth-century commentator Haribhadrasuri, practices like false weights and measures and adulteration were forbidden on religious grounds. In the seventh agna of the Jains written in Prakrit—*Uvasagadasao* (The Religious Profession of an Uvasaga)—a list is provided of the activities considered immoral. The Holy Quran too prohibits the use of false weights and false measurements. The list includes buying and selling of stolen goods, stealing, trade in banned goods, false measurements and dealing with fictitious goods. Cruelty to animals, including maiming, overloading and deprivation of food and water, was also considered immoral.

The main aim of the Indian philosophy of economics was to take both the individual and the society towards peace and happiness. The doctrine of *sukharthi samyato bhavet* (a person during the period of happiness should be self-restrained) is significant. In *Agmas Sutrakritanga* (direct preaching of Mahavira), man is classified on the basis of desire, accumulation and a tendency to indulge in violence.

The ancient Jains were agnostics, and within the broad stream of Hinduism, there were several heterodox currents that asserted a predominantly atheistic view. Hieun Tsang, the Chinese chronicler who travelled extensively in India during the seventh century AD, described the merchants of Benaras as being mostly unbelievers. He also wrote about arguments and debates amongst the followers of different Buddhist groups. Amongst the intellectuals of ancient India, atheism and scepticism must have been very powerful currents that required repeated and vigorous attempts at persuasion and change. By the fourth century AD, some of the most fascinating series of debates on what constitutes the scientific method had been produced: How does one separate our sensory perceptions from dreams and hallucinations? When does an observation of reality become accepted as fact, and as scientific truth? How should the principles of inductive and deductive logic be developed and applied? How does one evaluate a hypothesis for its scientific merit? What is a valid inference? What constitutes a scientific proof?

In the quest for the truth, the Upanishad seers concluded that Brahma is the Reality. Whatever is in existence is all Brahma. Brahma is the only one and there exists nothing other than it; reality is non-dual. He who sees plurality or believes in duality, undergoes the process of death again and again. The *Aitareya Upanishad*[2] explains that there was only one soul before creation. It thought to itself, 'I should create divisions of the Universe (lokas)' and with this thought, it created different worlds. According to *Chhandogya Upanishad*,[3] the real cannot be created from the unreal. In the beginning, there was nothing else excepting the monadic real. It desired to multiply itself and manifested itself in many forms.

The Buddhist philosophy rests on three existential concepts of impermanence (anitya), suffering (dukha), and no-self (anatman). The human is constituted by five aggregates (skandha) which flow together and give rise to the impression of identity and persistence through time. There was a general agreement that there is no soul that resides within the human body and leaves it at death, like the driver of a bus who gets off at the end of the journey. There is only the aggregation of components, which is caused by the previous moment and causes the next. In Mahayana[4] Buddhism, this term was extended to apply to all appearance that arises from Shunyata, and is therefore devoid, empty of self. The Sarvastivadi school of Buddhism (believing in the doctrine that all is real) considers the existence of a substance dependent on itself and not emanating from an external single source such as Brahma.

According to Jain philosophy, all substances have objective existence. They do not depend upon any external reality for their existence. Just as the existence of sentient entities is independent and real, equally independent and real is the existence of non-sentient entities. The real entities of both—sentient (jiva) and non-sentient (ajiva)—constitute the Universe.

The Universe is without beginning and endless with respect to time. Sentience is not born of non-sentience nor is non-sentience born of sentience. The Jain philosophers believe that whatever is there in existence today existed in the past too and will continue to exist in the future. It is in the nature of fundamental reality that what was unreal a day before becomes real the following day and that which is real today may become unreal tomorrow. The basis of the creation of what we call the world is the process of transformation. There are only two constituents of the world, sentient and non-sentient. The rest are all their extensions.

The ultimate essence of philosophical thinking lies in the integrated trinity concerning the substances that are fit to be known (gyeya), fit to be abandoned (heya) and fit to be accepted (upadeya). From the Sankya standpoint, matter is fit to be abandoned and soul is fit to be accepted. From the Buddhist standpoint, suffering and the cause of suffering are both fit to be abandoned. And emancipation from suffering and the way of being emancipated from suffering are fit to be accepted. Jain philosophy endorses abandoning of matter and acceptance of soul.

INDIAN SCIENCE

The scientists of the ancient tradition discovered the capability of the human mind to settle into a state of deep silence while remaining awake, and therein to experience a completely unified, simple, and unbounded state of awareness, called pure consciousness, which is quite distinct from our ordinary waking, sleeping, or dreaming states of consciousness. In that deep silence, they discovered the capability of the mind to become identified with a boundless, all-pervading, unified field that is experienced as an eternal continuum underlying all existence. They gave expression to the self-sufficient, infinitely dynamic, self-interacting qualities of this unified state of awareness, and they articulated the dynamics by which it sequentially gives rise to space-time geometry, and subsequently to all the distinct forms and phenomena that constitute the universe.

According to Vedic science, as the Supreme Creator creates the cosmos, the creative potency descends among the created beings to assist the Supreme Creator in manifesting the material worlds. So, it is believed that the Supreme expands Himself and also creates positions within the material cosmos which are taken by co-creators or demigods who assist in creating and maintaining the material manifestation.

There is a descending process of acquiring knowledge by which we understand the mysteries of life. It is the information provided by the Supreme Creator that descends through the ancient sages and scriptures, and His pure representatives. In this way, we can learn about the Universe and its purpose rather than trying to understand it only by analysing minute cells and parts of the cosmos, which is the way of modern science. Our great Indian mathematician of the twentieth century, Srinivasa Ramanujan, said, 'For me God, zero and infinity are interrelated and integrated. Each new theorem is one more piece of the infinite to fathom.'

Vedic scientists classified the material world into four elements—earth (prithvi), fire (agni), air (maya) and water (apa). To these four elements was added a fifth one, ether, or akasha. According to some scholars, these five elements (pancha mahabhootas) were identified with the human senses of perception—earth with smell, air with feeling, fire with vision, water with taste and ether with sound. Later, the Buddhist philosophers rejected ether as an element and replaced it with life, joy and sorrow.

Indians saw two energy sources in the environment, namely, the solar energy flux and geomagnetic energy flux. The science of environmental bliss (vastu shastra) aims to control the flow of these energies by selecting a proper direction and alignment of objects. By understanding the direction of energy flow, one can easily relate North and South to the geomagnetic organic flow and East and West to the solar energy flux. It is believed that if there were an imbalance between the directions or the energy flow, the resultant energy would be negative energy, which would then result in environmental aggression, creating disharmony among humans residing at that particular space.

Shulba Sutras (The Rules of the Cord) is the oldest source of the geometrical concepts. Appendices to the manuals of ritual (*Shrauta Sutras*) include the oldest known formulation of geometrical theorems, developed in the context of Vedic altar-building. The first decimal system and the oldest names of 'astronomical' numbers such as quadrillions and quintillions are recorded in ancient Indian texts.

The theory of origin of animal life, particularly of man, was correctly understood by the ancient thinkers. The *Vishnu Purana*[5] states that 'the aquatic life precedes the monkey life' and that 'the monkey life is the precursor of the human life'. The same theory was explained in an interesting way by the ten incarnations (dashavatara). The *Chhandogya Upanishad* described evolution as the manifestation of the Supreme Spirit (atman). In ancient India, medical science made advances in the areas of plastic surgery, extraction of cataracts, and dental surgery. The oldest treatise dealing with surgery is Shushruta's compendium, *Shushruta-Samahita*. Atraya and Charaka were great Indian medical practitioners.

India also has a fair share in the development of technologies, particularly the distillation of perfumes, the making of dyes, the extraction of sugar, and the smelting of metals. Glass was manufactured in India from the third century BC.

In the fifth century, Aryabhata gave the theory that Earth was a sphere. Aryabhata's main work, known as the *Aryabhattiya*, was translated into Latin in the thirteenth century. That's how European mathematicians learned methods of calculating the areas of triangles, volumes of spheres, and square and cube roots. Aryabhata also wrote about eclipses and the Sun being the source of moonlight a millennium before Copernicus and Galileo.

In the sixth century, Varahamihira gave five classical principles (siddhantas) of astronomy—Surya, Romaka, Paulisha, Vasishtha and Paitamaha. These principles laid the foundation of Greek (Alexandrine) astronomy.

Mathematics is the science to which Indians have contributed the most. Decimal system, place notation, numbers 1 through 9, and the ubiquitous 0, are all major Indian contributions to world science. In Brahmagupta's treatise written in the seventh century, we read about positive and negative quantities. The tradition continued till very recently through Srinivasa Ramanujan (1887–1920). Jagadish Chandra Bose (1858–1937), C.V. Raman (1888–1970), M. Visvesvaraya (1860–1962), Satyendra Nath Bose (1894–1974), and Subrahmanyan Chandrasekhar (1910–1995).

INDIAN PHILOSOPHERS

The first phase of the journey into the realm of Indian philosophy includes the Vedas, the Brahmanas, the Aranyakas and the Upanishads. In the next phase come the Buddhist Pitakas and Jatakas. In the third phase come Jain

Agamas and the literature expounding them. In Agamic literature, nine great treatises are mentioned.

The first great treatise is *Naisarp.* It contains the knowledge of designing a village protected by thorny fences or earthen walls (Grama); a village in the vicinity of mines (Akara); a big city (Nagar); a port (Pattan); a place which has exit and entrance by both land and sea (Dronamukh); a place where there is no other village within a long distance (Mandap); a capital city (Skandhava) and buildings (Griha).

The second great treatise is *Panduka.* It contains knowledge of mensuration, weights, etc., in relation to agricultural products, as well as knowledge of the production of grain and seeds.

The third great treatise, *Pingala,* is on aesthetics, mainly dealing with the adornment and beautification of ladies and gents as well as horses and elephants.

The fourth great treatise is *Sarvaratna.* It contains a description of the origin of the fourteen jewels of the universal monarch, out of which seven belong to the one-sensed living beings (ekendriya) and seven belong to the five-sensed beings (panchendriya).

The fifth great treatise is *Mahapadma.* It contains knowledge of textile manufacturing of all kinds of white and coloured clothes.

The sixth great treatise is *Kala.* It contains the knowledge of describing and foretelling the auspicious and inauspicious events of three past and three future years. It also contains the knowledge of one hundred different kinds of crafts and the knowledge of threefold occupation of public benefit, namely, defence, agriculture and commerce.

The seventh great treatise is *Mahakala.* It is on geological topics such as the mining of iron, silver and gold and also on technology of manufacturing gems (mani), pearls (mukta), crystals (sphatika) and corals (pravala).

The eighth great treatise is *Manavaka*. It is a great work on military art, techniques and strategies containing the knowledge of preparing warriors, armours and weapons as well as war strategies and penal policies.

The ninth great treatise is *Shankha*. It is a treatise on drama, poetics and instrumental music containing the knowledge of the techniques of dance, plays and poetical works.

Maharishi Patanjali's *Yoga Sutra*, written around 200 BC, is one of the central texts of yoga. In 195 concise statements, Patanjali defines yoga and its core components. The classical Sanskrit definition of yoga as Yogacittavrittinirodha is 'to block the patterns/modifications of consciousness'.

The mechanism of the conscious mind (mana), its development and its problems are psychic subjects. The journey on the path of yoga begins with restraining the activities of the mind. It starts with the ordinary state of consciousness and concludes in the state of Supreme Soul. There are many other branches—Raja Yoga, Hatha Yoga, Laya Yoga, etc. They furnish us with a detailed description of the reactions prompted by emotions and instincts.

The Indian ethical literature is also very rich. Thiruvalluvar's *Kural* is the most renowned. It is eulogized as a directory of a code of conduct and ethics for humanity. Written in Tamil more than 2000 years ago, the *Kural* consists of 1330 couplets under 133 chapters, each comprising ten couplets. The chapters fall under three major heads: Virtue, Wealth and Love. The first part, *Arathuppal* (On Virtue), describes the greatness of the individual man. The second part, *Portutpal* (On Wealth), is the largest with seventy chapters (700 couplets) covering the essentials of life in society. The third and last part, *Kamathuppal* or *Inbathuppal* (On Love), portrays the victory of the inner self. It is accurately called *poyyamozhi* or 'the book that never lies'.

Kundakunda, Umasvati and Siddhasena Divakara are three thinkers whose basic ideas set the trend for later thinkers. Kundakunda belonged to the second or third century AD. He was a pioneering Digambara thinker from South India. A total of eighty-four works on various themes are ascribed to Kundakunda, of which fifteen are extant. Three of these, all written in the Prakrit language, may be said to be philosophical masterpieces. These are the *Pancastikayasara* (Essence of the Five Existents), the *Pravacanasara* (Essence of the Scripture) and the *Samayasara* (Essence of the Doctrine).

The *Pravacanasara* is an elementary work dealing with the Jain substances (excluding time because it does not occupy any spatial points) and the fundamental truths, to which two additional categories are added, namely the meritorious and non-meritorious acts related to Karma (punya and paap).

The *Pravacanasara* is an insightful work whose three sections clearly delineate its scope: knowledge, the objects of knowledge, and conduct.

The *Samayasara* is an illuminating work dealing with the nature of the soul and its contamination by matter, and whether the soul's intrinsic nature is in any way affected or changed through Karma bondage in so far as it is the doer of activities. An attempt is made to reconcile these problems, solutions to which depend on the standpoint from which one approaches the issues.

Both morality and dharma are useful for a society. There is a natural relationship between the materialistic world and the world of sentience. This relationship generates illusion or attachment. Many complex problems of the world are the result of attachment and infatuation. Kundakunda gave us the principle of distinguishing or discriminating (bhedvigyana) in order to demolish the citadel of attachment.

Umasvati is famous for the first Jain work written in Sanskrit, called the *Tattvarthasutra or Tattvarthadhigama-sutra* (Mnemonics on the Meaning of the Fundamental Principles). He lived in the fourth century AD. Of the five works ascribed to Umasvati, the *Prasamaratiprakarana* (Treatise on the Love for Tranquillity)—which deals with ethical issues and is addressed to ascetics and householders—and the *Tattvarthasutra* are philosophically important.

The *Tattvarthasutra* contains a series of aphorisms, divided into ten chapters, which are understandable only with a commentary. The value of the work is evident from the fact that throughout the history of Jain philosophy, every major thinker has written a commentary on it. Until around the tenth century, the Digambara thinkers, such as Alankarrika (eighth century) and Vidyanandin (ninth century), took centre stage. They wrote in a difficult style and hardly any research related exclusively to their writings has been done.

Siddhasena Divakara lived in the fifth century AD and he wrote in Sanskrit and Prakrit. He wrote in Prakrit the *Sammaisutta* (Mnemonics on Proper Understanding; in Sanskrit, *Sanmatisutra*), dealing with the seven Jain standpoints, knowledge and the objects of knowledge. Siddhasena also wrote twenty-one short compositions, each consisting of thirty-two verses (and simply called the 'thirty-twos'), on a variety of themes, including eulogies to Mahavira, critiques of Buddhist and Hindu schools, and an exposition of Jain concepts.

Adi Shankara (788–820) was the most famous Advaita (literally non-dualistic) philosopher, who spoke of a spirituality founded on reason and without dogma or ritualism. The Advaita School is of the view that knowledge (jnana) of man's true nature is liberation. Bondage arises from ignorance (avidya) of man's true nature, and therefore, removal of ignorance roots out this bondage. Liberation is nothing more or less than man knowing his true nature. This true nature is his innermost essence, the Atman, which is nothing other than Brahma. He who knows this, not merely has bookish knowledge, but through his own experience, is liberated even when living.

Shankara's theology maintains that discrimination needs to be developed in order to distinguish the true from the false and knowledge (jnana) from ignorance (avidya). Shankara proposed that while the phenomenal universe, our consciousness and physical being are certainly experienced by us, they are not true reality, but are rather maya. He opined that the ultimate truth is Brahma, the single divine foundation, which is beyond time, space, and causation. While Brahma is the efficient and material cause for the cosmos, it is not limited by self-projection, and transcends all binary opposites or dualities, especially such individuated aspects as form and being.

We must pierce through a hazy lens to understand our true being and nature, which is not change and mortality, but the unmitigated bliss for eternity. If we are to understand the true motive behind our actions and thoughts, we must become aware of the fundamental unity of being. How, Shankara asks, can a limited mind comprehend the limitless Atman? We must transcend the mind to become one with soul-consciousness.

Shankara denounced caste and meaningless ritual as foolish, and urged the true devotee to meditate on god's love and to apprehend truth. His treatises on the Upanishads, Bhagwad Gita, and Vedanta Sutras are testaments to a keen and intuitive mind that did not want to admit dogma but advocated reason. His main lesson was that reason and abstract philosophizing alone would not lead to liberation (moksha). It was only through selflessness and love governed by discrimination (viveka) that a devotee would realize his inner self.

Hemachandra (1089–1172) systematized the Shwetambar tradition of Jainism. He did insightful analysis of other philosophical views in his *Anyayogavyavacchedika* (Critique of Other Schools). His treatise on yoga (*Yogashastra*), dealing with Jain ethics, is an exemplary work.

Abhayadeva, in the eleventh century, wrote scholarly commentaries on the Jain canonical works. In his commentary on the *Sthanangasutra*, a canonical text which is a compendium of Jain doctrine, ethics and cosmology, Abhayadeva discussed epistemological issues concerning the nature of knowledge, in particular its foundations, scope and validity.

In the twelfth century, Vadidevasuri wrote the excellent *Syadvadaratnakara* (The Ocean of Manifoldness). This is a commentary on his own work on knowledge and standpoints, inspired by the work of the ninth-century Digambara thinker Manikyanandin.

Yasovijaya (1624–1688) was an intellectual giant, praised not only for his acumen as a logician, but also for his vast knowledge of Jainism and other traditions. He is credited with up to one hundred works, including an attack on the great logician of Navya-Nyaya, Raghunatha Siromani (early sixteenth century), and a commentary on a work by Vidyanandin.

In 1760, Acharya Bhikanaji founded the Terapanth, laying stress on the thirteen (Tera in vernacular) religious principles, namely: (1) five Mahavratas (great vows), (2) five Samitis (regulations) and (3) three Guptis (controls or restraints). Terapanth avoids worship of idols. The practice of regulating the entire Panth by one Acharya has been a characteristic feature of the Terapanth and an example for emulation by other Panths. All monks and nuns of the

Terapanth scrupulously follow the orders of their Acharya, preach under his guidance and carry out all religious activities in accordance with his instructions.

In its history of a little more than 200 years, the Terapanth had a succession of only ten Acharyas. Apart from founder Acharya Bhikanaji, Acharya Jeetmal (the fourth Acharya) and Gandipathi Acharya Tulsi (the ninth Acharya) were outstanding missionaries and much loved torch-bearers of the great spiritualistic tradition of India.

In 1949, Acharya Tulsi[6] launched the Anuvrat Movement to uplift human life and revitalize the rapidly crumbling moral and spiritual values among the people, irrespective of caste, creed and colour. The movement has been striving to infuse with new life people degenerating fast into what T.S. Eliot[7] aptly calls 'living shadows inhabiting the great wasteland'.

Acharya Tulsi began his mission by carefully drawing up a code of conduct for all individuals in society. The code consisted of atomic or small vows (anuvrats), urging the individuals to pledge themselves willingly to observe them. The Anuvrat Movement strives for the middle path, steering clear of the two extremes of absolute ascetic life (mahavrats) and unbridled materialism, which result in moral indolence. The voice of the movement has by now permeated the masses, focusing their attention on the importance of self-restraint.

THE ROAD AHEAD

When we look ahead, we need to realize that some principles are meant for all times, while some are relevant only for a specific period. The word 'new' does not mean a radical change nor does the word 'ancient' mean preservation of everything that existed in the previous age. The permanent principles remain useful for a long period. The principles formulated for a specific period need to be altered even before they degenerate into conservative practices.

The twentieth century has gone and the twenty-first century has arrived. In every age, one comes across both the good and the bad. The weakness of the twentieth-century man was that he was more concerned about his own generation, neglecting the interests of the future generation. His comfort-oriented outlook and tendency to sow the seeds of destruction in the name of development were highly dangerous.

The present world needs a balanced mix of intellectual and spiritual growth. Only through spiritual development can the concept of development be balanced. There are five dimensions of the concept of development: (1) How does development affect an individual? (2) How does development affect society? (3) How does development affect various life-forms? (4) How does development affect environment? (5) How does development affect the world?

In order to strengthen the balanced concept of development, there are similarly five dimensions requiring effort: (1) materialistic, (2) economic, (3) intellectual, (4) moral, (5) spiritual. The main cause of an unbalanced concept is an incomplete system of education. The modern system of education is fully concentrated on enriching knowledge and earning one's livelihood. The important aspects of learning—to live together and with others, and learning to be one's true self—are almost neglected. The result is that while knowledge is increasing and economic development is taking place, peaceful coexistence and the identification of the inner wealth are being lost sight of. This situation has also paved the way for the evolution of this book.

Intolerance is a propensity that triggers violence. Just as industrialization is adding to global warming, so is our own intemperateness increasing. The individual, social, racial, communal and international problems are increasing on account of heated-up brains. We will have to find out the principles of cooling and calming the brain. It is only possible through spirituality.

The first step would be contentment, which means demarcating or fixing limits. Today every country longs for absolute sovereignty and economic supremacy. This ambition becomes the cause of its increased aggression and violence.

Similarly, if a religious creed or cult, having a fundamentalist approach, wants to make its ideology and lifestyle spread limitlessly, it becomes instrumental in triggering other people's aggressiveness and augments violence. Hence, for keeping tempers low and keeping intolerance, conflict and agitation below ignition point, national sovereignty needs to be confined within legitimate limits and there needs to be universality of religion through education.

The false conceptual understanding of economics gets implanted in the human mind from the very beginning. The conceptual belief that 'wealth is the be-all and end-all of life' becomes so dominant that familial bonds, human relationships and social commitments become secondary. Accumulating wealth becomes the sole objective of a person's life. The root of the problem is that while considering the utility of money, we are not taking into consideration other needs of life.

Desire or passion is an inborn human tendency. From this standpoint, passions or desires may be said to be the prime factors in life. But, because desires are fulfilled by wealth, wealth becomes most important in life. At the same time, without limiting or restricting desires through self-restraint, both desire and wealth become dangerous. As man lives in the materialistic world, he searches for solutions to his problems only in the materialistic world. However, the fact is that the root of the problem is not matter, nor does it lie in the external world. It lies within us, in our passions that distort our worldview and conduct. What is needed is that we should investigate the root cause and find solutions—both inside and outside. The external aspect of our strategy to solve a problem is the environment and the inner one is passion.

For purifying the instincts of desire and wealth, Dharma becomes the most important thing in life. Here, we do not want to identify Dharma with any creed. Dharma in the form of morality and spirituality is not connected with any creed. Although everyone is endowed with intuition, which is the inner consciousness, yet as one attaches more importance to wealth and materialistic objects, one's externally oriented consciousness is more active, and hence, one always tries to perceive reality only through it. It is because of this that most of one's decisions are incorrect. In order to take the right decisions, one needs to develop one's power of intuition or inner consciousness.

As a means of building an equitable, sustainable order, both the economic systems—socialistic and capitalistic—have not delivered. In our view, both socialistic and capitalistic systems are examples of extreme thinking. What is needed is a search for a middle path in which individual property is not banned completely and at the same time, there is no unrestricted or unscrupulous freedom for the accumulation of wealth. The crying need of the present age is the fixing of limits for both accumulation and individual ownership. The cornerstone of Indian culture has to be, 'Do not amass inessential wealth and do not cause suffering to others in trying to achieve your happiness.'

In our view there are fourteen main constituents of culture: (1) social order and milieu; (2) philosophy of economics; (3) system of governance (political apparatus); (4) politics; (5) foreign policy; (6) trade policy; (7) ideals of secularism; (8) philosophy of religion; (9) sciences; (10) schools of philosophical thought; (11) education; (12) language and literature; (13) arts; and (14) expression of human emotions and impulses. However, culture exists as a whole. When we ponder over its development and impact on human society, we cannot divide culture.

Indian ideas of mind and consciousness have permeated the rest of the world through music, yoga, mind-body medicine, and spirituality. Recently, Indians have excelled in information technology. Besides, India has demonstrated that democracy is a feasible ambition even for cultures and societies that are not familiar with it and that a large, multireligious, multicultural society can live together as a single political unit.

We conclude this chapter with the premise that much of our culture is a basket of accumulated beliefs and conditioned or acquired behaviour. Every generation is conditioned from before their times. It then learns its behaviour without thinking. It has codes of conduct and behaviour projected on it without even being aware that it is unconsciously performing to the expectations of others and reacting when its needs and expectations are not met.

Without even being aware of what is going on, we have been and we continue to be unconsciously manipulated. We are supporting extras in a play of consciousness that has been written and directed by other people, the society and the system. How do we become the directors of that play? The baggage of life that youths carry is fairly empty. But, buried in the genetic memory, waiting for the right environment, the right moment, are the patterns, the memories of our ancestors and the whole history of who we already are.

If life is seen as a spiritual pilgrimage, it is intellectually unknowable, because to journey is to do, and to know is to separate yourself from that which you already are. You are the dream, the dreamer, and the act of dreaming. Your pain comes from the fact that you have not realized this. In the next chapter, we talk about this pain and develop an understanding of what we are looking for, what we already are and what is it that strives to seek expression in us. Once we make that path open, we create a thousand pathways out of a seeming chaos.

2

The Evolutionary Process and Pain

> *Seven sins: wealth without work, pleasure without conscience, commerce without morality, worship without sacrifice, politics without principle, knowledge without character, and science without humanity. A society and culture free of these sins would be a society without violence.*
>
> —Mahatma Gandhi

COSMIC PRINCIPLE

In the first chapter, we discussed the evolution of Indian culture and tried to define and conceptualize it. In this chapter, we move on to the next question: What is it designed to accomplish? How is it positioned in the overall scheme of things? How is it approached and orchestrated? And perhaps most importantly of all, what is its future if development is essentially concerned with human needs and their fulfilment in the final analysis.

There are many different ways to perceive and define development. People have a variety of needs—to breathe, bond, eat, love, create, procreate, recreate, work, and the like—that must be satisfied if they are to function effectively in society and survive. This gives rise to a complex set of social, economic, scientific, artistic, educational, recreational, spiritual, technological, political and environmental requirements. How these requirements are dealt with in specific situations and in particular parts of the world is what development in general—and the development of culture in particular—is all about.

In order to address requirements as difficult and demanding as these, governments, corporations, foundations, and local, regional, national and international organizations use models of development, or have them in mind, when they make decisions about a variety of public and private matters. These models range from general notions concerning the fulfilment of human needs to highly sophisticated devices to address this issue in a systematic, sustained and coherent manner. What could be the central theme of such a model? Is there a principle?

Every civilization saw the connection between human beings and the Universe in a different way. Some saw the connection as anatomical, some as psychical, and some others as both. Parts of the Universe were thought of as parts of the human body and mind. The Universe was understood as a macrocosm.

Conversely, parts of the human being were thought of as analogous to parts of the larger Universe. The human being was understood as a microcosm. And as both the Universe and the human being actually existed, this macrocosm-microcosm relationship was considered as existing naturally.

The process by which living things, as we know them, have come into existence is, in the fullest sense, a creative process. It has created new aspects, that hold great potential. It has produced growth, movement and appetite; striving and effort, joy and pain; consciousness and conscious self-criticism.

Creative causation is the idea that physical causes produce their effects as an artisan produces his artefacts. In the world as we conceive it, natural causation has a creative aspect, at least in a very simple and commonplace sense. We can say that these are two sides of the same reality.

Natural teleology says that all changes in Nature are made for a purpose. But the only purpose we know anything about is the human purpose. To this end, we often ascribe a human aspect to purely natural events. For instance, the assumption that the plant breathes in carbon dioxide so that we may have oxygen to breathe. When we say that the course of natural history is towards maximum goodness, we are expressing the idea of moral progress as a natural law. The Universe itself may not have any goals, but people certainly do, and this is reflected in many descriptive concepts.

If we extend such ideas, we find that we are investing the whole of Nature with more and more human characters. For instance, the ancient Greeks and Romans saw omens of the future in the flight of birds, in the shape and markings of the entrails of sacrificed animals, in the eclipse of the sun or the moon, or in the appearance of a comet. Behind all this lay the vague notion that man's place in Nature was different from that of any other animal. The cosmos existed for his sake and hence anything out of the ordinary must have some special message for him. Some of this has survived in our popular superstitions, such as notions of lucky and unlucky days or numbers, or that a black cat crossing one's path brings bad luck. Modern science has abandoned all such ideas and has seen the Universe as a mechanism completely independent of humankind except insofar as mankind modifies it.

JIVA AND AJIVA

In the tsunami-affected Nagapattinam and Andaman and Nicobar Islands, the devastation that took place was heart-rending. What kind of a message was Mother Earth giving? Why is it that so much destruction, pain, suffering and death occurred? What was the purpose? Was it just another example of man being at the mercy of an unforgiving cosmos, or revenge being taken by the Earth for the environmental damage inflicted by humanity? Or was it fate or even a punishment from God Almighty?

The Universe is constructed from a multitude of materials. It is dynamic in form and shape due to the innumerable processes and interactions between these materials and structures. To the human, however, in his need to establish his place and purpose in the Universe, the most important material is biological and the most important process is evolution. How can a human learn to understand himself, an understanding that is vital to his survival?

The reality is made up of two eternal principles, jiva and ajiva. Both jiva and ajiva are eternal; they never came into existence for the first time and will never cease to exist. Jiva consists of an infinite number of identical spiritual units. Ajiva (that is, non-jiva) is matter in all its forms and the conditions of existence, namely, time, space, and movement. The whole world is made up of jivas trapped in ajiva; there are jivas in rocks, plants, insects, animals, human beings, spirits and so on.

Science has revealed that the human body is made up of millions and millions of atoms. The differences between one human being and another, and between any living being and non-living being, are all determined by the sequencing of a few atoms. Any contact whatsoever of the jiva with the ajiva causes the former to suffer and therefore existence in this world inevitably means suffering. Neither social reform nor the reform of individuals themselves can ever stop this suffering. The only way to escape from suffering is for the jiva to liberate itself from the human condition, from human existence.

From the cosmic perspective given by Mahavira, our planet can be seen as a living organism which has many parts that make up the whole. Her waters are like our blood, the land masses and plates are like our muscles, and all of us, including animals and insects, are like cells that move within her body. None of us can sustain life without the all-important element of oxygen. The systems we have within us that help us sustain our lives are also present within her. The Earth has natural processes to break down nutrients, replenish depleted systems, re-grow injured or failing parts, warm herself when she is cold and cool herself when she is warm. She is able to heal just as we are able to heal. There is a power that lies within her that also lies within each and everyone of us.

Different cultures in the world have myths and legends of a time when all of humanity was united and was one with their source. Somewhere along the way that unity was shattered and the separation began. Whether it was the banishment from the Garden of Eden or some other event of legend and myth, man separated himself from God Almighty. Mankind then proceeded through centuries trying to figure out who God was. Is God the sun, the moon or the elements of the Earth? Think how many centuries were spent in just trying to figure out who God was and how we could make Him happy. How could we make Him love us and shower favour upon us? Should we sacrifice precious lives? So many lifetimes were spent in trying to figure out what would do the trick.

Ironically, the desire to please God began to separate us from one another as people began to take sides about who was right and who was wrong. Greek philosopher Empedocles (490–430 BC) identified the fundamental forces in the Universe with the gods of Love and Strife—Aphrodite and Ares. According to Empedocles, all matter periodically contracts and expands. Under the power of Love, everything unites until there is only The One—a divine and homogeneous sphere. Then the sphere dissolves under the rising power of Strife and the world is established in a series of stages until it reaches a state of complete dissolution. History then reverses itself, and the Universe gradually returns to the state of the irreducible sphere. This cosmic cycle rolls on repeatedly without beginning and without end.

The search for God was abandoned and humanity pressed forward on a new road called need. At the end of this road lay power and wealth. Those who did not desire these things and chose to search for something greater were blinded by religion and forced to believe in a God of man's own creation—a God personified with the best and worst of human traits and emotions. This was a God who was capable of love, but was equally capable of hate, judgment, condemnation, need, and desire. As these civilizations began to grow and conquer one another, they began to separate themselves from the Earth as well. There were no more thanks for bountiful harvests or a sense of reverence for the Earth or for the spirits of Nature. Oil was greedily sucked out from the depths of the Earth to fuel purposeless wandering. Man took but no longer gave.

History is full of instances when people connected to the land were destroyed with swords. Thousands of native cultures were lost to time in this pursuit of power, wealth and glory. Cultures which revered the land and lived in harmony with the Earth were destroyed with callous disregard for their ways of life. These were people who understood that they were linked to the land and if one was affected by suffering, pain or death, it inevitably affected the other. They understood and respected this age-old symbiotic relationship. But this sacred knowledge was all but lost through the centuries. The interconnectedness between the human, animal, plant and mineral worlds was ignored and disregarded by the arrogance of materialistic development. Human evolution got marred by a spiritual regression.

ETERNAL TRUTH

The eternal word, truth, wisdom or principle existed before the creation of the Universe, and continues to function in guiding the creative process. 'He has created the Heavens and the Earth with Truth.'[1] What is meant by Truth? It is the eternally abiding Reality. The ancient road of Reality has been here all the time; like minerals, rocks, or diamonds preserved in the mine, Absolute Truth abides forever. Reality abides forever, and keeps its order, like the roads in an ancient city. For instance, let's say a man wandering in a forest discovers an ancient city with orderly streets and enters it. Having entered it, he may take a rest, conduct himself like a citizen, and enjoy all the pleasures accruing therefrom. Neither does this man make the road along which he enters the city nor does he make various other things in the city. He just enjoys the *suchness* (phenomena of life) of things.[2]

In our planet, there is a battle being waged on the suchness of life. The folly of our past is most evident. Organized religions are being reduced to shrines. Our idea of who God is and who we are is at odds with the nicely compartmentalized notions fed to us by the priests and clergy of yesteryears. People are no longer satiated by the power, wealth and glory that were once all they desired. They are now asking the all-important question, 'Who am I and why am I here on this planet?' Is there, in essence, a process of releasing the old energies we allowed to fester within us and damage us? These old energies led to the illnesses and diseases that plague us still. Is pain an essential part of the evolution process?

Evolution is not a process that is meant to torture us, force us to suffer or cause us more pain. Instead, it is meant to develop us. The spiritual evolution occurring within us will trigger a chain reaction. We will begin to reach unity with each other, with Nature, with Mother Earth and most importantly, with God. Truth is the life, substance and continuity of all things. We tread on forces. Withdraw them, and creation would collapse. Human knowledge calls them forces of matter, but divine science declares that they belong wholly to the divine Mind, are inherent in this Mind, and so it restores them to their rightful home and classification.

Is this the second part to this equation—the micro changes forcing macro changes? Is Mother Earth also releasing the old energies that have caused illness and disease to the important parts of her being? Is she trying to restore the balance that once existed? It can be and is a painful process. As she restores her waters and rejuvenates her lands, we face death and destruction. Must not the Earth release these energies and bring balance once again? Not to punish us, but to prepare a world where we can experience our new-found joy. So that Mother Earth may reflect the joy that we have found within ourselves.

Dr Karan Singh, spiritual philosopher, puts preservation of the environment as a central tenet of global society in his book *I Believe*. He writes, 'Our ancient literature exudes a profound awareness of environmental values. The whole concept of sacred groves and rivers, springs and forests was designed to emphasize the fact that human beings were not divinely endowed with the freedom to exploit and destroy nature at will, but rather (were) a part of the natural environment which it is their duty to protect.' The *Bhoomi Suktam*, Hymn to the Earth of the Atharva Veda (XII.I), has a remarkably comprehensive statement of environmental values in its sixty-three verses. To quote just one verse:

Whatever I dig from thee, O Earth,
May that have quick growth again.
O purifier, may we not injure thy vitals or thy heart.

What good would it be if humanity were able to experience an inward joy in a world that could not reflect that joy outwardly? How could that joy be experienced in our lives if the basic necessities of life could no longer be sustained on this planet? What we must remember and focus upon is that as with the changes occurring within us, the end result is joy. Once balance is re-established, we will be able to truly enjoy all the fruits of Mother Earth's labour and appreciate the bountiful harvest she provides. Joy will finally live within us and within her. There is a need for the micro and macro aspects of life to finally evolve. Adhesion, cohesion, and attraction are properties of evolution. There is a thought-force that launched the Earth in its orbit and said to the proud wave, 'Thus far and no further.' (Job 38.11, Holy Bible).

MORAL LAW

Law or teaching is often an ambiguous concept, for there are laws that fetter as well as teachings that liberate. 'God has revealed the fairest of statements, a scripture consistent with promises of reward paired with threats of punishment, at which creeps the flesh of those who fear their Lord, so that their flesh and their hearts may soften to God's reminder. Such is God's guidance, with which He guides whom He will. And him whom God sends astray, for him there is no guide.'[3]

Man has been a tribal animal since he first walked erect more than four million years ago. Being a biped, he could not outclimb or outrun his predators. Only through tribal cooperation could he hold his predators at bay.

For two million years, the early hominid was a herd/tribal animal, primarily a herbivore. For the next two million years, the human was a tribal hunter/warrior. He still is. All of man's social drives developed long before he developed intellectually. They are, therefore, instinctive. Such instincts as mother-love, compassion, cooperation, curiosity, inventiveness and competitiveness are ancient and embedded in the human. They were all necessary for the survival of the human and pre-human. Since human social drives are instinctive, not intellectual, they cannot be modified through education. As with all other higher order animals, however, proper behaviour may be obtained through training.

What separates the human from other animals is intellect, the faculty of reason, which developed slowly over the four million years or more of human development. The intellect developed as a control over instincts to provide adaptable behaviour. Over countless generations, the human being has been nurtured by Nature to modify any behaviour that would normally be instinctive to one that would provide optimum benefit. This process may be called self-control or self-discipline, and is the major difference between the human and the lower order animals, those that apply only instinct to their behavioural decisions. Self-discipline, therefore, is the measuring stick of the human.

The more disciplined the behaviour, determined by intellect displayed by an individual, the more human he becomes. The less disciplined the behaviour, in response to instinct, displayed by an individual, the more he becomes like the lower order animals.

Worship is one of the fundamental drives of life. When people visit a place of worship, their minds rise over instincts, converging towards the divine as thanksgiving or as prayer to God. In turn their minds are conditioned to serve God in whatever form possible. True worship does not deal with what we do with our bodies (singing, kneeling, or praying), but consists of who we are, what our heart is feeling and what we can give to the needy. Here we would like to relate a unique story from Punjab, one in which spirituality resulted in a societal mission.

There is a rivulet called Kali Bein. Here, Guru Nanak Dev is said to have received enlightenment. Over the centuries it turned into a sewage-ridden, weed-choked drain. Baba Balbir Singh Seechewal, in partnership with the Punjab state government, undertook a mission to clean the rivulet. He organized people's participation in stopping the massive flow of sewage into the rivulet and cleaned a 160-kilometre long stretch over four years. On an average, 3000 devotees volunteered every day in the mission. Today one can enjoy in this rivulet the flow of fresh water released from the Tarkina Barrage. The revival of the rivulet has recharged the water table as the hand pumps that had become dry for the past four decades are drawing water again. Baba, with the volunteers, not only cleared the rivulet of weeds and hyacinth, but also built bathing ghats at five places. He also built a 100-kilometre long kutcha road on the bank of the rivulet. In major places of worship in India, on an average 500,000 people come every day for prayers. Normally, when we go to a religious place, we pray for our happiness and prosperity. At these places of worship, can we not write and display certain vows that transcend personal petitions? Vows such as:

I will be responsible for educating at least five students for three years.
I will activate at least one water pond in my neighbourhood or nearest village.
I will remove all enmity within my family and withdraw any court cases.
I will plant five fruit bearing trees.
I will not gamble and succumb to any addiction.

I will treat male and female children in my family equally in education.

I will lead from now onwards a righteous life free from corruption.

Even if ten per cent of the devotees take any one of these vows and practise them, it will bring great peace and stability to society. 'Blessed is the man who walks not in the counsel of the wicked, nor stands in the way of the sinners, or sits in the seat of scoffers; but his delights are in the law of the Lord, and on His law he meditates day and night. He is like a tree planted by streams of water, that yields its fruits in its season and its leaf does not wither. In all that he does, he prospers.'[4]

ETHICAL PRINCIPLES

In its evolution, the society has gone from being agricultural to industrial, and more recently, to being an information and knowledge society. In the agricultural and industrial societies, humans and machines dominated. In the information and knowledge society, intellectual capacity will dominate. Intellectual domination is represented by ideologies, principles and faiths. History has shown time and again that whenever paths of individuals, societies and nations cross each other, then human rights are violated. Has man, in his social life throughout history, achieved evolution and exaltation? Is human society really undergoing evolution and will it reach a fully evolved state in future? If it is undergoing evolution, what is that ideal society, or, as Plato would say, that utopia of man, and what are its peculiarities?

Can we afford to close our eyes to the future and say that history inevitably moves on an evolutionary course? Is evolution in Nature imposed by time? Is the ship of time voyaging on an evolutionary course without the slightest intervention of man and without any responsibility on his part? Did human beings in the past have no role as beings endowed with free will, freedom of choice and responsibility? Has the role of human beings in the past been secondary and subject to determinism or has there been no such determining force in the past? The present generation faces economic and educational deprivation, the scourge of caste discrimination, and denial of timely justice at affordable cost. It is a cauldron from which revolution will give birth to a standard human being.[5]

Who is a standard human being? How has he evolved? There has been indubitable progress of man in the matter of tools and implements of life. So much so that it is quite probable that man's technical and industrial progress will reach a point when he may destroy himself and alongside all his achievements in science and technology, his books, his learning and civilization. If no such catastrophe occurs, there is no doubt that the creation of tools may further advance to a stage that is not imaginable today. For man has made so much progress in his experimental understanding and knowledge of Nature that he has been able to conquer it and turn it into a docile servant. This is one aspect of human progress.

Another aspect of man's evolution, if it can really be called that, is in the sphere of social life and the structure of society. Human society has gradually been transformed from a simple structure into a complex one. In other words, in the same way as he has advanced in technical and industrial matters from the simple cars of yesterday to the present-day aircraft and sophisticated spacecraft, human society, too, has changed from a simple structure to an extremely complex one.

The structure of primitive and tribal societies was very simple. Every tribe would have a chief, who would divide the tasks among the people, and these tasks were few in number. But with the progress of science and technology, such division of work has become complicated because there are more tasks and more people to perform them. Compare the existing variety of jobs, tasks, professions and crafts with those of the societies of a hundred years ago. Or look at the degree of specialization at the administrative and scientific levels. In the past, a person was able to master all the sciences of his time irrespective of what non-scientific position they were holding in their early career—two such examples being Einstein and C.V. Raman.

But now the system of education has undergone such subdivisions that we have hundreds of specialists, who are not the least acquainted with other branches of science. Indeed, they may be quite unaware of even their existence.

This is a characteristic of our time, a quality that removes uniformity and homogeneity from among human beings and replaces it with differences and distinctions. For, as man creates work, work too builds up man. As a result, although we all are human beings living in one society, yet we seem to possess different natures, since everyone is dealing with a task which is unknown to the other, who is engaged in another task. Each one of us seems to live in a different world of his making.

THE GOLDEN RULE

Jain canons consist of twelve main agamas, texts which have been handed down through the ages. It is said that having climbed the tree of perfect knowledge, an omniscient Lord Tirthankar showered flowers of knowledge to enlighten his principal disciples, called Ganadhars. They collected all these flowers in the cloth of the intellect and wove them into the garland of twelve agamas. *Sutrakritanga Sutra* is the second agama. This agama describes non-violence, Jain metaphysics, and the refutation of other religious theories. It records, 'A man should wander about treating all creatures as he himself would be treated.'

For more than four thousand years, gurus have been preaching the Golden Rule as a suitable rule of conduct among men. Rules are tools designed to make us think and behave in ways that we might not be naturally inclined to. All rules should be considered in the light of the thinking behind them, and this rule's principle is one of selfless service to others. Rules teach responsibility, awareness, ethics and concern towards others, all of which should be manifested in our behaviour if they are to have any meaning or value.

The Golden Rule or the ethic of reciprocity is a fundamental moral principle which simply means treat others as you would like to be treated. It is endorsed by all the great world religions and is the basis for the modern concept of human rights. The Golden Rule is best seen as a consistency principle. It doesn't replace regular moral norms. It isn't an infallible guide on which actions are right or wrong; it doesn't give all the answers. It only prescribes consistency—that our actions towards another be in harmony with what we would expect from him or her. It tests our moral coherence. If we violate the Golden Rule, then we are violating the spirit of fairness and concern that lies at the heart of morality.

The Analects are a record of the words and acts of the Chinese thinker and philosopher Confucius (551–479 BC) and his disciples. In one such discussion, Tse Kung asks, 'Is there one word that can serve as a principle of conduct for life?' Confucius replies, 'It is the word shu (reciprocity): Do not do to others what you do not want them to do to you.' Meng Tzu, or, in Latinized form, Mencius (372–289 BC), called the The Second Sage in China, was a Confucian who based his entire system of thought on the concept of jen:

humaneness, humanity and benevolence. To this basic doctrine he added the concept of righteousness. Mencius wrote, 'Try your best to treat others as you would wish to be treated yourself, and you will find that this is the shortest way to benevolence.'

The *Anusasana Parva*, the final instructions from grand old man Bhishma, is a long interlude in the narrative of the Mahabharata. 'One should never do that to another which one regards as injurious to one's own self.' This, in brief, is the Rule of Righteousness. By acting in a different way, by yielding to desire, one becomes guilty of unrighteousness. In refusals and gifts, in happiness and misery, in the agreeable and the disagreeable, one should judge the effects by a reference to one's own self.

In the Third Book of Moses, called Leviticus, God spoke to Moses, 'You shall love your neighbours as yourself.' Jesus of Nazareth gave the sermon on a mountainside to his disciples and a large crowd. According to the Gospel of Matthew, this particular sermon is called The Sermon on the Mount. The discourse summarizes itself by presenting a formulation of the Ethic of Reciprocity—do to others as you would have them do to you.

Islamic scholar Yahia bin Sharaful-Deen An-Nawawi gathered forty-two of the sayings of Prophet Muhammad, may peace be upon Him. Each saying, or Hadith, is one of the great precepts of religion and is described by religious scholars as the axis of Islam. On the authority of Anas ibn Malik, the servant of the messenger of Allah, the Prophet said: 'None of you is a true believer until he wishes for his brother what he wishes for himself.'

Eusebius of Caesarea[6] (263–339) is often referred to as the father of Church history. He wrote a prayer to practice the Golden Rules, some of which are:

May I be an enemy to no one and the friend of what abides eternally.
May I love, seek and attain only what is good.
May I desire happiness for all and harbour envy for none.
May I never find joy in the misfortune of one who has wronged me.
May I never wait for the rebuke of others, but always rebuke myself until I make reparation.
May I reconcile friends who are mad at each other.
May I, insofar as I can, give all necessary help to my friends and to all who are in need.
May I never fail a friend in trouble.
May I be able to soften the pain of the
grief-stricken and give them comforting words.
May I respect myself.[7]

What is the real reason for this kindly consideration of others? There is an eternal law that we reap what we sow. So when we treat others the way we want to be treated, we know what we have set in motion and what we can expect in return.

THE LAW OF CONSEQUENCES

One consequence of the transcendent law underlying the cosmos is that the cosmos evidences order, regularity, and mutuality. All existences, great and small, are linked in a web of interdependent relationships. Every relationship has a certain polarity and order and there is a dynamic exchange between male and female, heaven and earth, mind and matter, subject and object, light and dark, being and not-being, this and that, myself and the other. The movement within and between beings in a relationship is the source of evolution. This motion is seen in the regular cycles of Nature, the changing seasons. In addition, interdependence is the basis for teachings which deny egoism and acquisitiveness while encouraging compassion and reciprocity. Each person is his neighbour; any distinction between me as subject and the other as object is illusory.

The Law of Consequences is not a static law. We constantly use it to set in motion new causes to improve our lot. The Law of Consequences is intimately tied up with the Law of Rebirth, sometimes called the Law of Reincarnation. Our consciousness has experienced many lifetimes on Earth in the past, and it shall live through many more in the future. In each of these past lives we have set various causes into operation, some of which are only now in the present life bringing their effects into manifestation. In Hinduism and Buddhism, these effects are called Karma. Hindus look at Karma as a debt of destiny. Buddhists look at Karma as conditional existence. Hinduism says we are paying debts from the past, and that we are also reaping rewards from the past. Buddhism says we are clearing bondage and liberating ourselves from the conditions of our existence.

The first thing we have to realize is the concept of destiny. Prophet Muhammad (peace and blessings be upon Him) has said, 'Whenever Allah desires good for His creation, He gives him deep understanding of the religion and He inspires him with righteous guidance.' In its simplest meaning, destiny is reflection of character. The traits of character that most often cause bad destiny are anger, fear, pride, hate, revenge, sensuality, selfishness, envy and intolerance. The first thing to do is to scrutinize our habitual line of thinking and see if we have any of these traits in our make-up, even in a small degree. If we find that we have, then we must go to work on them and gradually remove them. The two principal means of doing this are changes in thought and action, particularly towards others. Thought, however, is the more basic, and if we correct our habitual thought, we shall find that our actions almost automatically follow the revised pattern of thinking.

This brings us to a most important factor in the situation, namely, the creative power of thought. This power is the most fundamental and potent factor in human life. The saying, Thoughts are things, is startlingly true. Every time we think a thought, we are making a thought form which may become a living force. It floats in our sensations and becomes a part of our mental atmosphere, a part of our very life.

The next step in the activity of creative thought is that it clothes itself in the substance of desire and emotion. This step has two effects: first, it may lead to corresponding action; second, thought forms not calling for immediate action may be stored in the memory as patterns for future use. We have access to them at any time; thus they may eventually appear as physical realities in our environment, making it good or bad according to our thoughts. Therefore, if we wish to change our environment and our fortune, we must change our thoughts. By so doing, we will be making a new and good destiny.

The destructive desires and emotions such as anger, hate, revenge and resentment—but particularly anger—disrupt and disarrange the thought forms and the thought creations of good which we have previously made, and thereby delay their materialization. When we have yielded to anger or revenge, for instance, and dissipated some mental creation of good, the corresponding thought form configuration has to reassemble itself before materialization can proceed. This takes time and delays the period of a favourable change in our environment or general fortune.

How can one avoid harmful thoughts and desires and keep them out of one's mind? It seems almost impossible at times to keep them from slipping in. The answer is, thought substitution. It is based on the principle that two thoughts cannot occupy the mind at the same time, and is similar to the principle of physics that two bodies cannot occupy the same space at the same time. When we are bothered by a harmful thought, it is good to substitute it with another thought and concentrate on it so positively that the harmful thought cannot get in. This is simple and only requires practice.

When a child is empowered by the parents, he or she gets transformed into a responsible citizen. When the teacher is empowered with knowledge and experience, good young human beings with value systems take shape. When an individual or a team is empowered with technology, transformation to higher potential for achievement is assured. When the leader of any institution empowers his or her people, leaders are born who can change the nation in multiple areas. When women are empowered, society with stability gets assured. When political leaders empower the people through visionary policies, the prosperity of the nation is certain. When religion transforms into a spiritual force, the people become enlightened citizens with a value system.

INNER POWER

There is an Inner Power that defines the relation of man with himself. It is a stupendous factor in human life and the one upon which general success in life is most dependent. It is our personal link with the Universe. Therefore, we can see how powerful this inner, higher self is. It is omnipotent because it is a part of the Universe. It is the function of evolution to unfold it into a positive, dynamic omnipotence. This is what we, the embodiment of eternal consciousness, are gradually learning to do in our daily lives and by our succession of rebirths.

This Inner Power affects one's personality and daily life in this way: the eternal consciousness within, which is omnipotent and possessed of all wisdom as well, is constantly sending messages down into the conscious mind. These messages appear as intuitions, inspirations and original ideas. They tell us what it is that the higher self in its wisdom wishes us to do. If we follow these suggestions and put them into effect, the results in our lives will be constructive. Failure will be changed into success, the obstacles which have beset us will gradually disappear, and we shall find that everything begins to work together for good and for success in every department of life. One can most effectively receive these messages by quieting the conscious mind, and particularly by having quiet times for meditation so that the conscious mind is stilled and the Power can speak to us and we can hear it. The Power speaks to us and sends us mental messages all the time, no matter how active we are. Conscience is another of the messages of the Power, which we would always do well to obey. If we follow the directions of this Power, it will speak to us in ever clearer tones, gradually reshaping our lives and transforming our failures into successes.

We must cultivate a belief in the existence of the Inner Power and in its ability to transform our lives. This belief is the wire, the electrical circuit, which connects us with it. If we establish a clear connection between the Power and our conscious mind, the result will be so much better, because then the Ego can send its messages to us much more clearly and effectively. Disbelief in these things impairs the connection and in some cases even destroys it. Then we are left more or less without the conscious guidance and wisdom of the intelligence within and easily go astray, so that failure follows.

If we listen to and obey the suggestions and directions of the Power within, fear and anxiety are taken away and we gain poise, which is a large factor in material success. We lose our fear of both life and death. We know that all things are ordered with wisdom and that they will turn out well from the spiritual point of view.

We can, moreover, increase the good results by praying to the Power within—by talking to it, having conversations with it—because it is right there, nearer than breathing. It will hear us and provide the wise response. Some people call this praying to God; and it is the same thing, because it is the eternal consciousness. When praying we are making for ourselves a new, constructive destiny to neutralize and offset some of the debts of our past years and lives.

At this stage of writing, one aspect has emerged very clearly. Whereas the progress of the civilizations had brought certain types of material prosperity, it had also brought associated pain for individual, family and society. We would like to elucidate this through a dialogue we had based on our experience:

Kalam: Acharyaji, you are a fount of knowledge who purifies every soul that comes into contact with you.

Acharya: Kalam, God bless you for what you have done with your team. God Almighty has a bigger mission for you and that is why you are here with me today. I know our country is a nuclear nation now. The mission for you is greater than what you and your team have done, and it is greater than what any human being has ever done.

Kalam: Your suggestions would definitely help pave the way for peace. For at present more than 20,000 nuclear warheads with corresponding delivery systems are threatening humanity.

Acharya: The nuclear weapons are proliferating in tens and thousands in the world. I command with all the divine blessings, you and only you, to find a solution for making the same nuclear weapons ineffective, insignificant and politically inconsequential.

Kalam: This shall be my guiding light. The time has come for us to translate our thoughts on developing a peaceful, happy and prosperous society through the development of the family and the nation in the form of a book.

Acharya: Only a good individual who has been brought up in an environment of a good family will be able to realize his or her responsibility towards the nation.

Kalam: Such a citizen will adopt the principle 'Work with integrity and succeed with integrity.'

Acharya: Let us name our book *The Family and the Nation*. What do you say?

Kalam: Indeed, it is a beautiful message, Acharyaji. I can see the value system provided by my family as being as functional as a computer operating system. Whatever I do, it all moves on the pattern provided by my parents in my early life.

Acharya: Tell me more about your early life.

Kalam: During World War II in 1941, it was a difficult time for our family at Rameshwaram. I was a ten-year-old boy then. War had almost reached Sri Lanka and we could hear the boom of shells. Almost everything was a rarity, from food articles to other necessities.

Acharya: You lived in a joint family?

Kalam: In a large joint family, indeed! My father and his younger brother's families all lived together. Our family had five sons and five daughters, three of whom had families. In our house, at any time, there were three cradles made of sarees hung from the beam.

Acharya: What was the fundamental nature of your childhood?

Kalam: Happiness of a simple life! One day, my mother was performing her evening namaz. My sister and sister-in-law went close to the cradles to ensure that their babies did not cry and disturb my mother. As soon as the children in the cradles saw their mothers and felt their soft touch, there was a spontaneous gurgling laugh from them. The beautiful sight of the serene look of my mother and the happiness of the grandchildren in the cradles and their happy mothers filled me with great joy.

Acharya: You are blessed, Kalam. There is nothing superior in the entire world than to experience the happiness of such a divine family environment of prayer and the innocent smiles of the new-born kids. What was your routine in childhood?

Kalam: I used to get up at four in the morning, take my bath and go for my maths class. My mathematics teacher, Swamiar, would not accept students if they had not taken a bath. I would come back at 5:30 and go for namaz with my father and learn the Holy Quran in Arabic school.

Acharya: You wrote in *Wings of Fire* about your childhood enterprise. Tell me about it.

Kalam: The Rameswaram Road Railway station was about three kilometres from our house. The Madras-Dhanushkodi Mail would pass through the station without stopping as a war-time emergency measure. The newspapers meant for distribution in our locality were thrown from the running train to the platform in bundles. I used to collect the papers and was the first one to distribute them in Rameswaram town. Looking back, I realize how my parents and teachers had talked unobtrusively of the value of dignity of labour.

Acharya: I took up monkhood at the age of ten. You made me live my early childhood today. You are not a monk and yet you lived a life of austerity and abstinence. Where did it all start?

Kalam: One day during war time (1940), when all my brothers and sisters were sitting and eating, my mother went on giving me chapattis made of rationed wheat. When I finished eating, my elder brother called me to the side and scolded me, saying that I had eaten my mother's share. I rushed to my mother and hugged her. From that day onwards I am watchful of whatever comes my way. My mother's prayers have always followed me.

Acharya: The mother's heart is indeed the child's schoolroom. In the words of French writer Balzac, 'The heart of a mother is a deep abyss at the bottom of which you will always find forgiveness.'

Kalam, you are so firmly grounded in your spiritual value system. I read your book *Guiding Souls*. You are deeply religious and yet very secular in your outlook. Did this broad perspective also come from your childhood?

Kalam: When I was ten, three unique personalities would meet in our house—Pakshi Lakshmana Shastrigal, who was the head priest of Rameshwaram temple and a Vedic scholar, Reverend Father Bodal, who built the first church in Rameshwaram Island, and my father, who was an imam in the mosque. They would discuss the island's problems and find solutions.

Acharya: India has had this advantage of the mixing of minds for thousands of years. Throughout the world, the need to have a frank dialogue among cultures, religions and civilizations is now felt more than ever. This action of dialogue, Kalam, has to spread among families and society...

Generally the family is confused with man and wife. I am a monk, you are a celibate. How did your understanding of family evolve?

Kalam: During a recent trip to Meerut in Uttar Pradesh, I visited a family. The Sinha family consisted of three generations. I sat through kirtans with them. I found that they all enjoyed every verse that was sung and were bubbling with enthusiasm.

Acharya: What did you learn there?

Kalam: When I interacted with the family members, they told me that whatever they do, they do it for God. Their work was highly interlinked with divinity. For example, the gardener feels he is gardening to get the flowers for worshipping God. The decorator is doing the mission of beautifying the divine place. The kirtan group used the musical instruments to generate appropriate tunes for the songs in praise of the Lord. The divine rhythm emanated because they were singing the glory of God with passion. For the family head, all the family members and those assembled there were images of God. Regarding their profession, each member, whether undergoing education or a career, felt that the religious family environment had enhanced their performance in every activity and made them happy and contented.

Acharya: This type of joint family system exists in many places in our country in many religious environments. Thousands of devotees come to see me with their families. When I look at their lives, I find that their greatest happiness is family happiness.

Kalam: Gandhiji asked us to aim at complete harmony of thought and word and deed. Those who aim at purifying their thoughts generate harmony around them.

Acharya: Definitely, harmony in the homes will bring order in the nation and thereby peace in the world.

Kalam: Is not this process in place throughout the history of human civilization?

Acharya: History of human civilization is nothing but the evolution of human consciousness over billions of human lifetimes.

Kalam: Evolution is not restricted to biology. Ideas also evolve, as well as nations, technologies, indeed anything that changes. When used in a considered way, the idea of evolution connotes more than change. It implies a process which, as in biology, is uninterrupted and causal, and which appears to follow an overall trend.

Acharya: As humans we have evolved from Nature and we ultimately depend upon Nature for our survival. Until we understand what we are as humans and how we are connected to the Universe, it is impossible for humanity to be wise, and to evolve the knowledge to live in harmony with Nature.

Kalam: Our bodies were designed over the course of millions of years for living in small hunting and gathering tribes. Natural selection has not had time to change our bodies, nor minds, for coping with fatty diets, cars, chemicals, and life in the city. From this mismatch between our design and our environment arises much, perhaps most, preventable modern diseases. The current epidemics of heart disease and cancer are tragic examples. Damage to the environment is indeed the result of not realizing individual or family responsibility towards our planet.

Acharya: We fail to realize that if we destroy our environment, we are destroying what is in fact our larger self. Kalam, you are a man of science and you meet children, hundreds of them. How do you see the effect of modern gadgets, like computers and internet, on young minds?

Kalam: The computer has indeed changed the way children's minds process information and affects not only what they know but what they are capable of knowing. They are increasingly immersed in data-based forms of knowledge, limited to information transmissible in digital form. The modern culture is sacrificing the subtle, contextual and memory-based knowledge gleaned from living in a Nature-based culture, meaningful interactive learning with other humans, and an ecologically based value system.

Acharya: It is evident that one considerable source of beauty and health in all animals is the advantage which they reap from the particular manner of life to which they are destined.

Kalam: Acharyaji, what is the source of the pain humanity has suffered throughout evolution?

Acharya: Although most of the human race has left the hunter-gatherer stage of evolution, our emotions and our bodies are still equipped for that former lifestyle. The contrast with lifestyles in an industrialized society has brought problems for the human race.

Kalam: What are these problems and is there a way out?

Acharya: Our bodies have many physical capabilities but few of us make use of them. We no longer run, climb trees, ford rivers or dig in the earth to find food. Our bodies pay a price for our life of leisure. We grow fat, our arteries clog up, and our feet hurt.

Kalam: Why is there so much unhappiness and sadness in individuals? Why are there quarrels in families? Why is there conflict in society?

Acharya: Our Stone-Age minds are still equipped to carry out the seven deadly sins: greed, avarice, sloth, etc. Society makes laws and rules to prevent us from following our natural inclination of self-preservation and survival of the fittest. Most of us learn to behave ourselves but we develop unhappiness, neurotic tendencies, hypochondria, paranoia, lack of confidence and other ills that fatten the purses of psychiatrists.

Kalam: How can we be happy?

Acharya: The potentiality to do good is also the potentiality to do evil. What is needed is increased awareness and perception of the environment and increased ability to react accordingly.

Kalam: We have impulses and propensities coded in our genes and in the limbic systems of our brains as the result of millions of years of evolution. We also possess a freedom, through imaginative choice, to enact these impulses and propensities in countless ways. So existentially we need a code of ethics by which to order our behaviour.

Acharya: We are truly the changelings of possibility.

Kalam: Let's assume that an organization to teach cultural adaptation is to be created. What should it be like?

Acharya: It seems logical that such an organization must:

1) Factor anthropological history in industrialized society.
2) Identify the emotional and physical problems of people.
3) Seek out the available educational tools.
4) Point out the values of solving problems.
5) Disseminate this knowledge to the public.

Kalam: The relish for pleasure must be accompanied by temperance and decency.

Acharya: As human life continuously evolves and progresses, pain will also be proportional in the form of environment deterioration, natural calamities, new forms of sicknesses and, at the same time, revolution in science. We need a moral code or guideline of ethics to meet these challenges. Here, teaching of Jeevan Vigyan to the children will indeed prepare the young and strong generation to meet the challenges of growth.

Kalam: The biggest folly of modern man appears to be his being in conflict with Nature.

THE ETERNAL ORDER OF PROGRESSION

There is an eternity of knowledge before us; at most we receive but very little in this stage of our progression. The most learned men on this earth have only been able to obtain a small amount of knowledge in comparison to the vast store of information that exists. It cannot be exhibited by any individual to an extent greater than what people are able to comprehend. Consequently, knowledge must descend to our capacity to understand it.

Mankind is made up of elements designed to endure through eternity; they never had a beginning and never can have an end. There never was a time when this matter, of which each one of us is composed, was not in existence, and there never can be a time when it will pass out of existence; it cannot be annihilated. It is brought together, organized, and capacitated to receive knowledge and intelligence.

Harold Waldwin Percival (1868–1953) believed that a human being is made up of nature units that make up the body, its breath form or living soul, its conscious doer, and the Conscious Light, which is loaned to the doer. The state of being aware of Consciousness allowed one to know about any subject simply by thinking about it. Percival defined thinking as the 'steady holding of the Conscious Light within on the subject of the thinking'.

Briefly stated, thinking consists of four stages: 'selecting the subject; holding the Conscious Light on that subject; focusing the Light; and the focus of the Light. When the Light is focused, the subject is known.'[8]

Percival saw the human body as the plan of a changing Universe. 'Senses of the body are the ambassadors of Nature at the court of man; the representatives of the four great elements of fire, air, water, and earth, which are individualized as sight, hearing, taste, and smell of the human body.' The senses themselves do not see, hear, taste, smell or contact independently. They merely receive impressions from Nature and carry them to the breath-form, and the breath focuses them and correlates them so that they do their work through the smell of sense.

Only a small portion of the doer lives in the body. The entire doer is prevented from coming in because of the weakness, inefficiency and unfitness of the body. The embodied portion of the doer is limited in the exercise of its own power because of its own ignorance, indifference, sloth, selfishness and self-indulgence. It does not understand who and what it is, how it got here, what it has to do, what its responsibilities are and what is the purpose of its life. Because of indifference, it allows itself to remain in ignorance and be a slave of Nature. Because of sloth, its powers are dulled and deadened. Because of selfishness, of blindness to the rights of others and the need for gratification of its own wants, it cannot understand and feel its powers. Because of self-indulgence, the habit of giving way to its own inclinations, appetites and lusts, its powers are drained and wasted.

Because thinking is more real than the appearances of matter, it can demonstrate their relative unreality. It can deprive pain of its hurt, disease of its devastation and age of its withering. Thinking can call into existence objects like money and possessions, and it can create circumstances of employment and success. Such is the power of thinking. Many people use this power. They force themselves to think that their pain, disease, age, discomfort and poverty do not exist, are not realities, but are illusions. However, they want to get rid of them not because they are illusions, but because they are unpleasant; and they want to put in their place other, more pleasant illusions.

The result of such practices is self-deception and an increasing inability to distinguish illusions from realities, and the true from the false. While such people may intend to be honest, they blind themselves to the facts owing to prejudice and preference.

Man is beset, surrounded, submerged by illusions. All outside things are illusions. So are his appetites, pains and pleasures, dislikes and hatreds. They are elementals. He does not know his own feelings and desires, aside from their illusions. He does not see the people he thinks he sees; he sees only the thoughts which he creates of them. Therefore, if a thousand people see a man, no two would see him alike, because no two out of the thousand thoughts would be alike.

The doer in the human is limited in the exercise of its powers by slavery to Nature. The doer has made itself dependent upon the four senses of thinking, feeling, desiring and acting. It is unable to think of anything as apart from the senses or as different from what is reported by the senses. Its feeling is guided and ruled by sensations, which are Nature elementals that play upon the nerves. The human is thus shut off from the realms beyond the senses and is bound to the lowest states of matter on the physical plane.

Our civilization is indeed a study of the dire results of the loss of connectivity with the eternal. As mankind evolves, there are some, nevertheless, who lag behind, blinded by the desire of personal gain, by ambition and lust for power, so that today there are some who refuse the opportunity that for ages their souls have waited for. We—those of us who have achieved this perspective on worldly gain—and they—those who have not—have met in the past as in this life, and shall meet again in the future, and by our action today we are forging the links that shall help or mar their progress, as well as our own and that of all humanity. This is the pain inherent in the evolution process.

3

The Idea of Unity

> *Do good to parents, kinsfolk, orphans, the neighbour who is near of kin, the neighbour who is a stranger, the companion by your side, the wayfarer and those whom your right hand shall possess.*
>
> —Al Quran

WHAT LIFE SHOULD MEAN

In the preceding chapters, we have established the concept of human evolution as a refinement of the way we live and interact with one another, and the expansion of the eternal consciousness. In India, in Vedic, Buddhist and Islamic writings, the cosmic character of life is taken for granted. It is regarded as an inherent property of an infinite, timeless and eternal Universe. In Western philosophy, the idea that living seeds or spermata have been ever present in the cosmos was posited by the pre-Socratic philosopher, Anaxoragas,[1] as early as 500 BC. The law of biogenesis says that all life comes from life, and that each organism comes from one or two parents of its own species. It thus inherits its characteristics in unbroken lineage from its ancestors from the beginning of its species on Earth, and, if we accept the theory of evolution, from the beginning of all life on Earth.

This chapter deals specifically with the theme of unity. We begin with the unity of body and mind, and the various tasks and social roles that have to mutually support one another to build a unified community. We will then discuss ideas for unity not only of the community but of humanity as a whole. We will conclude with a spiritual declaration, celebrating the unity of all, a gift of grace and a manifestation of the Oneness of Ultimate Reality, which reconciles those who would otherwise be enemies.

By the turn of the twenty-first century, man had learned how to mass-produce knowledge. This new skill has been successfully tested in the environment of private business enterprise and market economy. Economic, social, cultural and all other human activities have become greatly dependent on knowledge, and the success of any society lies in harnessing it. But in what sense does knowledge exist? What is the relation of knowledge to truth?

Human knowledge is a subjective means of coming to grips with the world. It never captures the essence of Reality; it merely characterizes it according to our own purposes. In an ironic sense, we are epistemologically blinded to Reality by our own senses, which we take to be indicators of an absolute, independent world. Before we can judge the truth or falsity of a proposition, it must first make sense to us.

English poet William Blake (1757–1827) saw poetry as an attempt to make sense of the incomprehensible Real. The ancient poets animated all sensible objects with gods or geniuses, calling them by names and investing them with the properties of woods, rivers, mountains, lakes, cities, nations, and whatever their senses could perceive. Particularly, they studied the genius of each city and country, placing it under a mental deity. Religion as a system took it further and enslaved the earthly by attempting to realize the mental deities from their objects. Thus began priesthood, which chose forms of worship from poetic tales. At length religious authorities pronounced that God had ordered such things. Thus men forgot that all deities reside in the human heart.

The monistic theory of the Universe is that One is All, and All is One. Hinduism believes that one substance manifests itself as the seeming many elements of the material world. It also believes in a causal relationship between thought and circumstances.

The concept of Karma implies a cause and effect. Each of us is different and hence, lives differently. But we ourselves reap the results of our conduct. Good conduct breeds good results. The concept of Dharma means purpose in life. Each of us has a purpose in life. It calls for self-discovery to unravel the inner layers of our minds. The most important book of Buddhist literature, *Dhammapada,* says that our lives are shaped by our minds; we become what we think. Mind precedes all mental states; Mind is their Lord; they are all mind-made. If one speaks or acts with a harmful mind, trouble follows as the wheel follows the ox that draws the cart... If one speaks or acts with a harmonious mind, happiness follows like a shadow, never leaving.[2]

BODY AND MIND

The partnership of growth and development continues from the first days of life till the end. Body and mind cooperate as indivisible parts of one whole. The mind is like a motor, mobilizing all the potentialities it can discover in the body, thus helping it survive all difficulties. Our work is inspired by our minds. The development of our bodies is directed and aided by our minds. The mind is always engaged in governing the environment in such a way that the body can be protected from sickness, disease and death.

This is the purpose served by our ability to feel pleasure and pain, and to identify ourselves with good and bad situations. The feelings of an individual bear the impress of the meaning he gives to life and of the goal he has set for his strivings. Though feelings rule his body, they do not depend on his body; they depend primarily on his goal and the consequent style of life.

Baruch de Spinoza (1632–1677) contended that everything that exists in Nature/Universe is one Reality. There is only one set of rules governing the whole of the Reality which surrounds us and of which we are a part. Spinoza viewed God and Nature as two names for the same Reality that is the basis of the Universe and of which all lesser entities are actually modes or modifications. All things are determined by Nature to exist and cause effects, and that complex chain of cause and effect is only understood in part. Humans presume themselves to have free will, he argues, because they are aware of their appetites. However, they are unable to understand why they want something and act the way they do. Spinoza's argument goes like this: substance exists and cannot be dependent on anything else for its existence; no two substances can share the same nature or attribute; substance can only be caused by something similar to itself, something that shares its attribute; substance cannot be caused; substance is infinite; therefore there can only be one substance.

In 1929, Albert Einstein (1879–1955) was asked in a telegram by Rabbi Herbert S. Goldstein (1890–1970) whether he believed in God. Einstein responded: 'I believe in Spinoza's God who reveals himself in the orderly harmony of what exists, not in a God who concerns himself with the fates and actions of human beings.' Some of Spinoza's philosophical positions are: the natural world is infinite; good and evil are related to human pleasure and pain; everything done by humans and other animals is excellent and divine. Spinoza contended that an emotion can only be displaced or overcome by a stronger emotion. For him, the crucial distinction was between active and passive emotions. While active emotions are rationally understood, passive ones are not. He held that the knowledge of the true causes of a passive emotion can transform it into an active emotion.[3]

Gottfried Wilhelm Leibniz (1646–1716) variously invoked one or another of seven fundamental philosophical principles: (1) Principle of Identity/Contradiction (if a proposition is true, then its negation is false and vice versa); (2) Principle of Identity of Indiscernibles (two things are identical if and only if they share the same properties); (3) Principle of Sufficient Reason (there must be a sufficient reason for anything to exist, for any event to occur, for any truth to obtain); (4) Principle of Pre-established Harmony (a dropped glass shatters because it knows it has hit the ground, and not because the impact with the ground compels the glass to split); (5) Principle of Continuity (Nature makes no leap, everything evolves); (6) Principle of Optimism (the best is assuredly always chosen); and (7) Principle of Plenitude (the best of all possible worlds would actualize every genuine possibility and there is no reason to dispute Nature's perfection).[4]

Arthur Schopenhauer (1788–1860) investigated what makes man less than reasonable. He called this force Wille zum Leben or will-to-life. This force drives man to remain alive, feel desire and reproduce. This Will is the inner content and the driving force of the world, and has ontological primacy over intellect. Desire is prior to thought, and, in a parallel sense, Will is prior to being. It is similar to notions of purushartha or goals of life in Vedanta Hinduism.

In *The World as Will and Representation*,[5] Schopenhauer proposed that humans living in the realm of objects are living in the realm of desire, and thus are eternally tormented by that desire. Will is an aimless desire to perpetuate itself.

Desire engendered by the Will is the source of all the sorrow in the world; each satisfied desire leaves us either with boredom, or with some new desire in its place. The wild and powerful drive to reproduce causes suffering and pain in the world. Since the Will is the source of life, and our very bodies are stamped with its image and designed to serve its purpose, the human intellect is, in Schopenhauer's simile, like a lame man who can see, but who rides on the shoulders of a blind giant.

Man has always debated whether the mind governs the body or the body governs the mind, whether the individual shapes society or the society governs the individual. Philosophers have joined in the controversy and have taken one position or the other; they have called themselves idealists or materialists; capitalists or socialists; they have brought up arguments by the thousand; and the question still seems as vexed and unsettled as ever.

We see mind and body, individual and family, family and society, all as expressions of life: they are parts of the whole of life. Individuals and families function within the context of a community, which in turn functions within a larger society, the nation, and the world. There is a reciprocal relationship. The life of man is the life of a performing being, and it would not be sufficient for him to develop the body alone and then to develop family alone. To perform in life for a larger purpose is the central principle of the mind. The well-being of the individual and the family is bound up with the community's well-being, and likewise the community's well-being is inseparable from the peace and prosperity of the society, the nation and ultimately, the world. Religious precepts bind the community by teaching the virtues of cooperation, friendship, justice and public-mindedness. These create the spirit of unity by which a community can thrive and prosper.

INNATE INSECURITY

Alan Wilson Watts (1915–1973) defined religion as the relation of human beings to that which they regard as holy, sacred, spiritual or divine. He analysed the similarities and differences of themes, myths, rituals and concepts among the world's religions. In the field of what Watts called comparative religion, the main world religions are classified as Abrahamic, Indian or Taoic.[6]

The category of Abrahamic religions consists of the three monotheistic religions, Judaism, Christianity and Islam, which claim Abraham as part of their sacred history. The original belief in the One God of Abraham eventually became present-day Judaism. Christians believe that Christianity is the fulfilment and continuation of the Jewish Old Testament, with Jesus as the Son of God. Islam believes the present Christian and Jewish scriptures have been modified over time and are no longer the original divine revelations as given to Moses, Jesus and other prophets. For Muslims the Quran is the final revelation from God, with Muhammad as His messenger for its transmission.

There are a number of religions that have originated on the Indian subcontinent. These include Hinduism, Buddhism, Jainism, and Sikhism. The religion of the Vedic period is the historical predecessor of the Hindu religion. The Vedic and the Shramana traditions co-existed and influenced each other since pre-historic times. Jainism and Buddhism are a continuation of the Shramana tradition. Buddhism further diversified into Chinese and Japanese schools. Tao can be roughly stated to be the flow of the Universe, or the force behind the natural order. The flow of *Chi*, as the essential energy of action and existence, is compared to the universal order of Tao. Following the Tao is also associated with a 'proper' attitude, morality and lifestyle.

People who believe that their thoughts, experiences, and emotions are, as a matter of contingent fact, the only thoughts, experiences, and emotions that can be, are called solipsists. By analysing the three states of experience—waking, dreaming, and deep sleep—Adi Shankaracharya (788–820) established the singular Reality of Brahma, in which the soul and Brahma are one and the same. Ishvara is the manifestation of Brahma in human minds under the influence of an illusionary power called Avidya. The 'real' world is but an illusion in the mind of the observer. When the solipsist understands the maya or the illusion of the world, he escapes the mundane and reaches the state of everlasting bliss, realizing that he, the Self, is the whole Universe, thus making himself God.

In this model of Reality, Brahma plays a game of hide and seek with himself. In this game, called Lila, he plays the individual people, the birds, the rocks and forests, all separately and together, while completely forgetting that he is playing a game. At each Kalpa, he ceases the game, wakes up, applauds himself, and resumes it. So one of the main points in waking up and being enlightened is knowing that one is simply playing a game, currently acting as a human being, having an illusion of being locked within a bag of skin and separated from the whole of the cosmos.

The Buddha stated: 'Within this fathom-long body is the world, the origin of the world, the cessation of the world and the path leading to the cessation of the world.'[7] Though he did not reject the occurrence of external phenomena, the Buddha focused on the illusion of Reality that is created within the mind of the perceiver by the process of ascribing permanence to impermanent phenomena, satisfaction to unsatisfying experiences, and a sense of reality to insubstantial things.

Epicurus (341–270 BC) drew the conclusion that the existence of evil is incompatible with the existence of the gods, who care about mankind and bestow benevolence, knowledge and power. He believed that pleasure and pain are the measures of what is good and bad, that death is the end of the body and the soul and therefore should not be feared, that the gods do not reward or punish humans, that the Universe is infinite and eternal, and that events in the world are ultimately based on the motions and interactions of atoms moving in empty space.[8]

Most of man's strivings are directed towards a position in which he feels secure, where all the difficulties of life seem to have been overcome. In striving for the final goal of security, the mind is always faced with the necessity of making the goal concrete; of calculating whether 'security lies in this particular point; (whether) it is reached by going in this particular direction'.

All psychological mistakes are thus mistakes in choosing the direction of movement. The goal of security is common to all human beings; but some of them mistake the direction in which security lies and their concrete movements lead them astray.

CHILDHOOD CRYSTALLIZATION

In the first four or five years of life, an individual establishes the unity of his mind and constructs the relations between mind and body. He takes his hereditary material and the impressions he receives from the environment and adapts them to the pursuit of superiority. By the end of the fifth year, his personality has crystallized. The meaning he gives to life, the goal he pursues, his style and approach, and his emotional disposition, are all fixed.

These traits can be changed later, but only if he becomes free of the mistake involved in his childhood crystallization.

Just as all his previous expressions were coherent with his interpretation of life, so now, if he is able to correct the mistake, his new expressions will be coherent with his new interpretation.

A mind which has fixed its goal in a mistaken direction will fail to exercise a helpful influence on the growth of the brain. It is found that many children who lack the ability to cooperate show, in later life, that they have not developed their intelligence, their ability to understand.

According to Alfred Adler (1870–1937), in the first four or five years, a fixed style of life is adopted with corresponding emotional and physical habit patterns. Its development includes a larger or smaller degree of cooperation between mind and body; and it is from this degree of cooperation that we learn to judge and understand the individual. In all failures, the highest common measure is a small degree of the ability to cooperate. Since the mind is a unity and the same style of life runs through all its expressions, all of an individual's emotions and thoughts must be consonant with his style of life. If we see emotions that apparently cause difficulties and run counter to the individual's own welfare, it is completely useless to begin by trying to change these emotions. They are the right expression of the individual's style of life, and they can be uprooted only if he changes his style of life.[9]

Here lies the basis for our educational outlook. We must never treat education as a uniform offering of knowledge: it must cater to the unique mind of the student receiving it, in the way his mind has interpreted his experiences, in the meaning it has given to his life, and in the actions with which it has answered the impressions received from his body and from the environment. This is the real task of education.

TWO MISSIONS

In India, there are 220 million people below the poverty line and 300 million young citizens who are below twenty years of age. This is the innermost core of India that is in need of social and economic development in an ambience of peace and harmony. India has a road map in the form of India Vision 2020 document.[10] This encompasses five important areas that are vital to bring in sustainable prosperity and help this vulnerable section of our population: agriculture and food processing, education and health care, information and communications technology, infrastructure development (including networking of rivers), and providing urban amenities in rural areas (PURA). These areas need to be taken up simultaneously. When the villages prosper, the states prosper. When the states prosper, the nation prospers.

India is a country of plurals. We have multiple faiths and cultural traditions. The vision of celestial love (puja) is central to the Indian heart. And it is very earthy, almost carnal. This has a long tradition in vernacular literature, going back to the devotional poems of Chandidas, and those of the Bhakti movement of Sri Chaitanya and others. This earthiness is essentially the same as that appearing in the devotional lyrics of Kabir or Mirabai, and goes back even further in the tradition of Bhakti Yoga that permeates the special Indian vision of celestial love.

As if refocusing the original vision of celestial love, we made 'Unity of Minds' our foremost mission. 'Let there arise out of you one community, and inviting to all that is good, enjoining what is right, and forbidding what is wrong: those will be prosperous. Be not be like those who are divided amongst themselves and fall into disputations after receiving clear signs: for them is a dreadful penalty.'[11]

THE NATURE OF FAITH

Faith is something one 'believes in'. It serves a major evolutionary purpose and has been an essential part of human nature since time immemorial. When shared by members of a group, faith strongly supports that group's internal cohesion. It strengthens that group's capacity to cope with the challenges of a hostile environment, and to compete successfully with other groups animated by different faiths. If you believe in nothing, if you question everything, then where are you? You are like a ship adrift, without a destination. You have a crew but no captain, no pilot, no compass, and no charts. You may end up in different waters from where you began, but to what purpose? What was the voyage for? The matter of faith changes all that. You know where you are going. If you in your lifetime get there, at least you were going in the right direction—and your faith may give you the assurance that somehow, the voyage isn't over, you will continue in some other form. Faith lends meaning to an otherwise meaningless existence. It makes the whole matter of life worthwhile.

All religions are based on faith, but not all faiths need to be religious, at least in the sense of requiring adherence to a recognized religious persuasion. Religion teaches one to be altruistic, but traditionally that spirit of altruism has applied primarily to members of one's own group. All too often, believers have chosen to show their enthusiasm for their chosen faith by fighting other groups. Our tolerance for this kind of religious zeal is diminishing.

The world over, poverty, illiteracy, unemployment and deprivation are driving forward the forces of anger and violence. These forces link themselves to some earlier real or perceived historical enmities, cruelties, tyrannies, injustice, inequality, ethnic issues and various forms of religious fundamentalism. Individually or severally, they lead to outbursts of extremism worldwide, including world wars. The feelings of hatred feed on themselves, leading to an inferno. The world has witnessed and is witnessing today the unsavoury acts of certain misguided sections of society. We have to address ourselves to the root causes of such phenomena for finding lasting solutions, and promote peace through unity of minds.

The unity of minds is basically a humanist precept. It resides comfortably at the heart of the humanist perception; anywhere else, inside any old-fashioned belief in a God that favours some groups over others, it is an unfamiliar element. It troubles the true believer with the contradiction between tribal suspicion of outsiders and the thought that the outsider is a human being like him. Like the sand in a pearl-bearing oyster, such a doubt can irritate the ranks of the faithful into gradually, over many generations, perhaps, expanding the ambit of their faith in a pan-humanist direction to include all humanity.

We are sceptical about the old-fashioned faiths that require uncritical acceptance of the doctrines and dogmas of the major established religions. Faith is more a state of mind that leads people to believe something—it doesn't matter what—in the total absence of supporting evidence. Faith is indeed capable of driving people to such dangerous recklessness that it can be a kind of mental illness.

We insist that there needs to be some point of departure, some base point, if we are to establish direction and purpose to our lives. And accepting this has to be a a matter of faith. You cannot go back indefinitely, asking 'why' to every preceding answer like a curious but annoying child. You have to stop somewhere. For us the base point is that all humanity is our home team.

As human beings we must accept the need for some kind of faith. As with some computer games, we arrive on the scene facing a blank map of our universe. We spend our lives travelling in as many parts of that universe as possible, conducting our explorations rationally and even, when possible, scientifically, to make sure we illuminate them as accurately as possible. Thus we do away with the darkness wherever we go; the islands and seas and continents are revealed, one by one. The longer we live and explore, the greater the revealed area. Meanwhile, the areas that are still dark recede. But they never go away entirely; we can never see the totality. We have to assume certain things about those dark areas that persist outside the range of our experience. We draw on what we have learned, so that we can make these assumptions as plausible and credible as we can, aiming to maximize the likelihood that they will prove accurate. The more we learn, the better we become at this kind of probability assessment. But we can seldom be totally certain of anything. Faith in humanity is not a bad place to drop your anchor in this day and age. It is the starting point for the unity of mind.

DIVERSITY IS NATURAL

We are social animals. Our genes are predisposed to absorb the language patterns of people around us during our initial years. While we learn what is to become our native language, we also absorb the values of our peers. This process is natural, biological and inherited; it is part of our nature, the common inheritance of humans everywhere. The equality of all persons, male and female, rich and poor, of any race, class, or caste, is proclaimed in the scriptures of all faiths. This is true despite the conventions of many cultures that discriminate between people on the basis of caste, class, race or sex. Regrettably, such discrimination is also on occasion supported by certain conventional interpretations of passages from sacred texts. Yet with the development of a more refined religious consciousness, all forms of discrimination are being overcome, and interpretations of religious texts that have traditionally fastened on to discriminatory attitudes and practices are being shown to be erroneous.

Until quite recently, till information and communication technology opened up boundaries, social groups regarded their own internal ethical standards as absolute, universal and right. Validated by their religious leaders, their moral guidelines formed an integral part of their worldview. Other groups' standards, where they differed, were usually seen as aberrant, abnormal, and wicked, the result of worshipping false gods. Thus ethical standards were part and parcel of a general human condition in which language, religion and culture operated together to divide groups from one another while reinforcing solidarity within the group.

We now know enough about human origins and human social evolution to develop a new perspective on the question of where ethics come from. Once we accept the fact that morality, like language and religion, is culture-specific rather than universal, the scales fall from our eyes and we see the world around us in a different and humbler light. We see that there is no morality in Nature as such; there are only forces and processes that have operated over millions, even billions of years, to bring about our present condition. God, at least the God we used to worship, can now be recognized as a device of the human imagination. Morality, it follows, is equally a human invention. We are our own saviours and redeemers. It is up to us, just us alone, both to develop the ethical principles guiding our conduct, and, through common sense or acceptance by the majority, to validate them.

Equality is a social state of affairs in which different people have the same status in certain respects. There are different forms of equality, depending on the persons and social situations in question. For example, one may consider equality of the sexes in opportunities for employment. In this, the people in question are men and women and the social situation is the search for a job. As another example, equal opportunity refers to the idea that all people should start out in life from the same platform and that all should have equal opportunities in life, regardless of where they were born or who their parents were.

The essential equality of all people is supported by the doctrines of the monotheistic faiths, that God is the parent of all humanity and that all human beings are descended from one pair of original ancestors, Adam and Eve. In Hinduism, Jainism, Buddhism, and Confucianism, this equality is grounded in the fact that Enlightenment, unity with the Absolute, or the realization of Goodness is available to all universally. Distinction among people, therefore, should be based only on their conduct, morality, level of spiritual education, and attainment.

MULTIFAITH SOCIETY

The underlying tenets of Indian civilization, which is termed as a Hindu society, cannot be easily defined. There is no unique philosophy that forms the basis of the faith of the majority of India's population. Hinduism is highly diversified in its theoretical premises and practical expressions. The Rig Veda, Upanishads and the Bhagwad Gita are described as the sacred texts of the Hindus.

The Vedas and Smritis speak highly of equality and brotherhood—*Vasudhaiva Kutumbakam* (One World One Family). The entire world is a family, was the motto of Vedic civilization. The Vedic age was more liberal in providing equal status to the people. Jainism, Buddhism, Christianity, Islam, Sikhism and other indigenous Indian religions also preach the principles of brotherhood and equality.

Naturally, over a period of time, certain groups have monopolized certain trades. Due to vested interests born out of economic insecurity, certain groups started compartmentalizing people. Society was segregated into social divisions, ghettos of isolation and exclusiveness. This has been the case in every nation and society.

Economic factors notwithstanding, religion remained a way of Indian life. For the majority of Indians, religion permeates every aspect of life, from commonplace daily chores to education and politics. Secular India is home to Hinduism, Islam, Christianity, Buddhism, Jainism, Sikhism and innumerable other religious traditions.

The personality and teachings of Gautam Buddha, the founder of the Buddhist faith in fifth century BC, illumined the lives of people in a big way. There are strong lines of similarity between Buddhism and the basic teachings of Hinduism. Buddhism is based on the principle or the law of impermanence. According to this, everything is subject to change, although some things may last longer than others. The other basic principle of Buddhism is the law of causation, according to which nothing occurs on account of pure chance. Besides natural forces, it is Karma which leads to the occurrence of all events. The popular notions of the indestructible soul and the cycle of rebirth emerge from these two basic philosophies.

Buddha advocated the Middle Path, in which he offered a balanced, harmonious way of life, steering between two extremes of self-indulgence and total abstinence. Buddhism rests upon four Noble Truths: (1) suffering is universal; (2) it is caused by desire and yearning; (3) suffering can be prevented and overcome; and (4) eradication of desires can lead to removal of suffering. To prevent suffering, one has to conquer craving and desire, and this conquest leads to the attainment of nirvana or complete enlightenment.

Jainism as a religious tradition was established by Mahavira. He preached the Jain philosophy around the same time that Buddhism began. Like Buddhism, Jainism was a reaction to the practices prevalent in Hinduism at the time. The underlying philosophy of Jainism is that renunciation of worldly desires and self-conquest leads to perfect wisdom. This faith believes in total abstinence and asceticism as practiced by the Jinas (conquerors) and the Tirthankars (ford-makers or supreme sanctified Jain masters). Tirthankars help people cross over from the material to the spiritual realm, from bondage to freedom. Followers of this faith accept the popular gods of Hinduism but they are placed lower than the Jinas.

The focus of this religion has been purification of the soul by means of right conduct, right faith and right knowledge. This faith also enunciates complete non-violence and the Jain monks can be seen with their nose and mouth covered by a cloth mask to ensure that they do not kill any germs or microbes while breathing. Today, Jainism has more than 3 million adherents in India and finds wide acceptance because of its philosophy of sympathy for all living beings.

The Arab traders brought Islam to India in the early eighth century, but it was not until the twelfth century that it found its roots in the Indian subcontinent. Unlike Buddhism and Jainism, which emerged from Hinduism, the concept, customs and religious practices of Islam were unique to this faith, which professed universal brotherhood and submission to Allah or God Almighty.

The Mughal rulers in the sixteenth and seventeenth centuries helped spread Islam in India. In its first phase, Islam was forceful. But the mystics of Islam, or the Sufi saints, helped in spreading the message of peace and universal love. The spirit of brotherhood propounded by Sufi saints and preachers like Kabir and Guru Nanak Dev helped in loosening the rigidity of the caste system. The interaction of the two faiths led to a synthesis of Hindu and Islamic elements in almost every sphere of life and culture. After an initial period of conflict and confrontation, today the two religions have accommodated and enriched each other.

The Sikh religion emerged during the early sixteenth century in the state of Punjab in North India. Guru Nanak Dev, who was born a Hindu but was inspired by the teachings of other religions, including Islam, began to preach the message of unity of religions. According to him, the basic teachings of both the faiths were essentially the same. Guru Nanak Dev attracted many followers. His disciples came together to form a new religious tradition called Sikhism.

Sikhism propounds monotheism: the worship of one God. It also opposes the caste system and believes that all men are equal. However, the ideas of Karma and rebirth from Hinduism are accepted and many Sikh practices are similar to those of the Hindus. Intermarriages between the two communities are also common. Nevertheless, the Sikh community has its own unmistakable identity. Though the Sikhs constitute less than 2 per cent of the Indian population, they have become a distinct element in the configuration of the Indian religious tradition and the Indian society.

INDIAN STEREOTYPE

A vibrant India is rapidly emerging onto the global economic platform. For the first time, a democratic country with a population of over one billion will be actively participating in growth, trade and investment. This has significant implications for the world economy and the process of globalization. India must assume new roles and responsibilities to manage the impact in a way that benefits its development as well as that of the world.

When we talk of globalization and of a borderless world, the focus so far has largely been on the movement of goods, capital and financial and logistical services. There is as yet no clear framework for the movement of people. On the other hand, developed economies are becoming more restrictive with respect to immigration and the movement of labour.

MIND OVER EMOTION

Indian philosophy places a tremendous confidence in the power and supremacy of the mind over emotion, and affirms an overweening assurance that the human mind, through its understanding of oneself and one's fellow men, is able to adjust itself to the most unfavourable circumstances and triumph over them. Tulsidas chose *Ramacharit Manas* as the title of his translation of the great epic Ramayana, giving centrality to character over events. Here, character is meant in the sense of the illumination of understanding developed and cultivated through knowledge. A mellow understanding of life and of human nature is, and always has been, the Indian ideal of character, and from that understanding other qualities are derived such as pacifism, contentment, calm and strength of endurance, which distinguish the Indian character at its best. Strength of character is really strength of mind, according to Vivekananda. When a man has cultivated these virtues through mental discipline, he can be said to have developed character.

Thinking Process

This brings us to the powerful influence of Indian 'fatalism'. This fatalism is nothing but a clear perception of, and a consistent attitude towards, the iron laws of cosmic necessity, understood as the laws of Nature, the dictates of destiny or the will of the Almighty. Whether or not such an attitude makes people lazy and pessimistic, as is sometimes claimed, it certainly endows them with a capacity to face adversity with fortitude. In as much as happiness depends to a large extent on our ability to negotiate misfortune, there is something to be said for this attitude. After all, it is the function of a religious ethos to enable its members to find peace under any circumstance. The obverse side of this, of course, is that being at peace with oneself means acceptance and acceptance means inertia.

Once you get into a frame of mind where you accept everything, you tend to become incapable of the youthful enthusiasm for progress and reform without which there can be no change. Is it a bad thing? It is a vexing question with no easy answer. The more we study history the more difficult it is to say what has brought more misery to mankind: the desire for change or the reluctance to change. Good or bad, the fact remains that Indian civilization represents an old culture of ancient people who are too conscious of the receding horizons of perfect happiness and hence are wary of striving for the unattainable. As Kabir puts it:

Maya mari na maan mare, Mar mar gaye shareer;
Asha trishna na miti, Kah gaye Das Kabir.
(Neither the mind dies nor its delusions,
Only the body dies;
Hope and desire never perish,
So said Das Kabir.)

However, when we talk of these aspects, we must be careful not to lapse into racialism and begin to imply that these attitudes are racial features innate to the Indian people. These are only cultural characteristics. This becomes obvious when we look at Indians who were brought up in other cultural surroundings. They often exhibit a worldview alien to the Indian temperament. Our 'national' character, therefore, is a product largely of our conditions. The Indian capacity for patience, for example, is a product of our family conditions. The training school for developing this virtue is the big family, where daughters-in-law, brothers-in-law, fathers and sons learn this virtue daily by learning to coexist with one another. In the big family, where a closed door is an offence, and where there is very little elbow room for individuals, one learns, as much by necessity as by parental instruction, from early childhood the need for mutual toleration and adjustments in human relationships.

MASTERS OF ETHICS

True ethics is universal. The ethical goes back to a single principle of morality, namely the maintenance of life at its highest level, and the furtherance of life. Reverence for life is fundamental to all thought. All material and spiritual values are values only in so far as they serve the realization of that reverence in practice. While compassion is the noble feeling that serves as the motive force for all ethical conduct, there is another, still deeper factor underlying moral behaviour. The Bhagwad Gita actually teaches us about that factor. But we tend to be distracted by the overt ethical message of the Gita and often fail to realize that the Gita is not interested in just sermonizing on how we should treat one another but addresses a matter of ultimate importance, namely, the realization and salvation of the self.

What is this realization? The answer lies in the great insight provided by ancient Indian mysticism which affirms the unity of individual souls of all beings with the Universal Soul. According to this concept, all that is of the nature of soul belongs to the Universal Soul. Man carries the Universal Soul within him. And because the Universal Soul dwells in all beings, it finds its own self again in all beings, in the life of plants as in the life of gods. This is the meaning of the famous dictum 'Tat twam asi' (That thou art thyself) of the Upanishads. This same insight pervades all religious traditions. For instance, the Ahimsa commandment in Jainism not to kill and not to harm does not arise from a feeling of compassion, but from the idea of keeping one's self undefiled by worldly greed and selfishness. It belongs originally to the ethic of becoming more perfect, not to the ethic of interpersonal action.

The nineteenth century saw the birth of some great sages and saints who were animated by a sense of the spiritual unity of the Universe and stood as exemplars of a way of life that reflects that sense. Among them were Sri Ramakrishna, Swami Vivekananda, Sri Aurobindo and Sri Ramana Maharishi. These great souls transformed the religious outlook of modern India in a healthy, positive way, and it can be said that as long as that influence is intact, the religious ethos of modern India will remain on the whole well-balanced.

TRAFFIC WITH THE PAST

The serenity and peace among the lamas living in monasteries high up in the mountains is in amazing contrast to the hurry and distraction of modern life. Their deep faith in the reality of eternal values and their earnest endeavour to live, individually and socially, in the light of that faith seems almost ideal. On the other side of the spectrum is the modern youth's understandable reluctance to accept doubtful authority or uncritically follow half-understood traditions.

How can we deny that religions have confounded eternal truth with temporal facts and have become a sort of traffic with the past. Serious thinkers who should know better are spending their time and energy in finding modern ideas in ancient texts or reading meanings into them which are not there. Unable to show the independent relevance of their own domain, men of religion have begun to turn tradition into a facet of modernity, to defend religion on the basis of the latest findings of science. We keep forgetting the untiring message that emanates from every single religious tradition: it is not scientific findings or philosophical arguments that can validate the spiritual dimension. The true test of the spiritual is the ethical. Goodness is the ultimate and only test. In the words of the Dalai Lama: 'The roots of all goodness lie in the soil of appreciation for goodness.'[12]

ENDURING PLURALISM

What is the unique feature of Indian civilization? Perhaps an emotional open heart and a tolerant mindset! Anthropomorphic conceptions that look upon God as king or conqueror, father or law-giver, the good shepherd or the righteous judge possessing to a transcendent degree the qualities of power and virtue that we most admire in human beings lie at the crux of all religions across the planet.

As we have to live on earth, the spectacle of an incarnate God may have great religious value, but a too sharply defined anthropomorphism makes for narrowness and intolerance and takes us into the realm of the absurd. Many overtly religious convictions, very zealously and sometimes violently held, tend to hide the central truth that God is Spirit and that the only real worship is that which is in spirit and truth.

Like religious thought everywhere, the Indian ethos is based on an awareness that our life is not of ourselves alone; that there is another, greater life enfolding and sustaining us. But the beauty of the Indian religious ethos is that it grants that our search for this greater self need not accept any particular creed as final or any particular set of laws as perfect. Religion can be practised in almost any number of different, equally valid ways. This essential pluralism of the Indian ethos explains the existence of many faiths in Hindu religion as well as multiple indigenous versions of other major religions. Not that there have not been lapses, deviations and even refusals, both in earlier times, and less forgivably, in recent times. But these are only aberrations. In the words of the sociologist Leela D'Souza, the real, enduring India is syncretic, pluralistic and tolerant.[13]

Against this backdrop the Acharya and I invited fifteen prominent religious leaders to the Acharya's abode in Surat. The result of this gathering was the birth of a historical declaration.

SURAT DECLARATION

When we worked on the concept of a conclave of multiple faiths, we studied the ten 'commandments' of Leonard Swidler,[14] a professor of Catholic thought and inter-religious dialogue at Temple University, to start a constructive inter-religious dialogue. The ten points are: (1) The purpose of dialogue is to increase understanding; (2) Participants should engage in both inter-faith and inter-religious dialogue; (3) Participants should be honest and sincere; (4) Participants should assume that other participants are equally honest and sincere; (5) Each participant should be allowed self-definition; (6) There should be no preconceptions as to areas of disagreement; (7) Dialogue can only occur between equals; (8) Dialogue can only occur where there is mutual trust; (9) Participants must be self-critical of their religious traditions; and (10) Participants must attempt to experience how the traditions of others affect them holistically.

We met swamis, maulvis, reverend fathers, spiritual leaders and hundreds of their devotees. We discussed how religions can help the movement towards the vision of a developed India. How the rich culture and civilizational heritage of thousands of years can be synergized with development in the modern world.

God has given man the faculty to think. He has commanded His creation to use the faculty to reach His image. This is the mission of human life. Science is a recent boon God has bestowed upon mankind. Science with reasoning becomes the capital of the society. Spirituality is a special quality God has given us. Our duty is to discover it and use it for the benefit of all.

Every religion has a central component—spirituality driven by compassion and love. Rationality and logic are intrinsic to science and spirituality. A spiritual experience is the goal of a deeply religious person whereas a major discovery or an invention is the goal of a scientific mind. If both the aspects are unified and amalgamated in our own patterns, we can transcend to a level of thinking in which unity is a cohesive concept. For this environment, the two major components—science and spirituality—have to interact. A peace prayer can be the foundation for both.

Peace Prayer

Oh Almighty, create thoughts and actions in the minds of the people of the nation so that they live united.

Oh Almighty, bless the people to take a path of life with righteousness as righteousness gives the strength of character.

Help all religious leaders of the country to give strength to the people to combat the divisive forces.

Guide the people to develop an attitude to appreciate different viewpoints and ways of lives and transform enmity among individuals, organizations and nations into friendliness and harmony.

Embed the thought 'Nation is bigger than the Individual' in the minds of the leaders and people.

Oh God, bless the people to work with perseverance to transform the country into a peaceful and prosperous nation.

SPIRITUAL WELLNESS

'How can I live through suffering and pain?' is one of the key questions asked in the spiritual dimension. Spirituality is not the same as religion. As a matter of fact, some people can belong to a religion and not have a very well developed spirituality. Spirituality is thought to pertain to the ultimate meaning and purpose of life. Each individual needs to find meaning and purpose in life, and to define a value system in which to operate. Spiritual wellness is achieved as each person's actions become more consistent with their values and their belief systems.

As you explore your spiritual path, you may experience many feelings of doubt, despair, fear, disappointment and dislocation as well as feelings of pleasure, joy, happiness and discovery. You will know you are becoming spiritual when your actions become more consistent with your beliefs and values. The spiritual goal of every religion is indeed an individual free of violence in mind and body, which leads to a peaceful society. Removal of poverty is one of the components for realizing peace.

REMOVAL OF POVERTY

We realize that 300 million young citizens who are below twenty years of age in India want peace, prosperity, happiness and safety. It is our responsibility as religious and spiritual leaders to carry out this mission of removal of poverty. Fortunately, there is a road map to go to the India 2020 of our national dream. That entails working intensively on five important areas that have been identified earlier. These are agriculture and food processing, education and healthcare, information and communication technology, infrastructure development, including networking of rivers and providing urban amenities in rural areas.

Removal of poverty means addressing several related elements such as removal of illiteracy and providing good governance. It it is vital to ensure that funds allotted for the poor and the earnings by the poor are not frittered away through corruption or other social evils. This is where the making of an enlightened citizen comes in. It acquires a moral, ethical and spiritual dimension. Therefore, another component for prosperity is religious and spiritual partnership. We have considered how this partnership can be developed.

NATION'S PROSPERITY

Religions are like exquisite gardens, places full of surpassing beauty and tranquillity, like sacred groves filled with beautiful birds and their melodious songs. Religions are also like islands, veritable oases for the soul and the spirit. If we can connect all these islands with love and compassion, in a 'garland project', we will have a peaceful, happy and prosperous India in front of us. Universal truths embodied in each religion are very similar and they will help to form a bridge, thus reinforcing basic unity. Another fact of today is that the intellectual gap between the opinion-maker class and the masses is rather big. This gap is best removed by increasing the knowledge base of every citizen in various vital aspects of their lives. As the number of enlightened citizens increases, the ability to cope with and overcome problems also increases. To achieve this, in addition to concentrating on education of the youth, there is also a need for a continual education of the adult population and senior citizens on the values of life and about the basic spiritual unity of all religions. In addition these values have to be reinforced in every citizen through specific projects, which can bring people together, irrespective of their social levels or religious beliefs.

GARLAND PROJECTS

To achieve the above we resolved to undertake five projects and activities: (1) Celebration of inter-religious festivals; (2) Multi-religious projects; (3) Education in and with the ambience of unity of religions; (4) Inter-faith dialogue; and (5) Creation of a national-level independent and autonomous organization managed by religious and spiritual leaders as well as scholars and enlightened citizens.

Inter-religious Festivals

Every month in all parts of India there can be a multi-religious gathering to convey the core message of the prayer of peace and about the basic truths contained in various religions. Such a prayer should be preceded by prayers from all religions practised in that part of the country by respective religious and spiritual leaders in the presence of the people. Each month the day selected could be a holy day from one religion. Regular conduct of such meetings by all religious leaders and people from different religions respecting holy days of other religions will send a powerful message. If possible, such gatherings can take place at religious places where persons from other religions also can gather on that day. People should also exchange pleasantries and sweets during these meetings, as is the practice in some parts of the country where unity of minds prevails. In addition, in order to spread the message of equality to everybody on that day, a langar (community kitchen and eating) can be arranged so that all people eat common food sitting side by side. We believe that if all the religious and spiritual groups build a strong connectivity, it is possible to turn these monthly meetings into mass movements for respecting each other's rituals and ways of life.

Multi-religious Projects

So far, religious groups have made many efforts towards the removal of poverty, but in isolation. We will launch a number of multi-religious projects in education, healthcare and water supply as well as entrepreneurship and employment to help the poor. People will see for themselves that multiple religions are working together for the common good. These efforts will elevate religions in the minds of the people and the nation will benefit.

Education for Unity of Religions

Religious educational institutions operating in different parts of the country should enrol some children from other religions and impart values such as religious tolerance and righteousness. The real purpose of religion and an understanding of the underlying unity of all religions should be embedded in the minds of the students. These children will foster a sense of peace and amity between themselves. Simple exercises to reinforce positive thinking can be carried out. In addition, specially designed value-based educational material should be given to the children. The same should also be disseminated through the media. It may not be necessary to begin an exercise to generate these materials, as a large amount is available in India and abroad. However, it may be necessary to search for it and shape it to suit our specific needs.

Inter-faith Dialogue

In addition to the above projects impinging directly on common people and citizens, it is also necessary to have a continual inter-faith dialogue between the religious and spiritual heads as well as scholars. This dialogue can address, among other things, a common code between religions, methods of creating a congenial atmosphere for various religions, and solutions for some of the burning problems of the society. Deliberations at inter-faith dialogues can be widely disseminated among people through various agencies of the electronic and print media. Models for these dialogues exist in some other countries as well. Maximum benefit may be derived from such knowledge-sharing in addition to finding our own unique methods.

Catalysing Action

The religious and spiritual leaders came to the unanimous conclusion that in order to pursue the above in a sustained manner for achieving speedy results, it is essential to set up a national-level independent and autonomous organization managed by religious and spiritual leaders as well as scholars and enlightened citizens. This organization will train persons in essential aspects of different religions, in methods of spreading love and compassion among people, in removing hatred as well as in the basic theory and practice of non-violence. This organization, being an independent entity, will also become a focal point and a catalytic agent for organizing the other projects listed above and in extending the necessary infrastructure for the expansion of the efforts into a national mass movement.

India can emerge as a developed nation by 2020 with its civilizational heritage and value systems spreading harmony and peace to the whole world. This 'Unity of Minds' can be achieved even while keeping intact the rich diversity of rites, rituals, ideas and beliefs amongst us and blending them with modern knowledge and skills.

The following distinguished spiritual leaders put their signatures on the Surat declaration: Shri Shri Balagangadharanatha Swamiji, the 71st head of Shri Adichunchanagiri Mahasamithi Math, located near

Bangalore; Dr Homi B. Dhalla, founder of the Zoroastrian Cultural Foundation in Mumbai; Bishop Dr. Thomas Dabre, secretary general of the Council of Catholic Bishops of India; Jagadguru Sri Sri Sri Shivaratri Desikendra Mahaswami, the 24th pontiff of Sri Suttur Math, Karnataka; Rev. Stanislaus Fernandez, archbishop of Gandhinagar; Swami Jitatmananda of the Ramakrishna order; Shiek-e-Tarigat Hadrat Syed Muhammad Jilani Ashraf, the 28th descendant of Hadrat Ghuthe-Azan Syed Abdul Qadir Jilani; Rev. Ezekiel Isaac Malekar of Judah Hymn Synagogue, New Delhi; Prince Huzaifa Mohynduddin, son of H.H. Dr Syedna Muhammad Barhanuddin, the 52nd incumbent of the august office the Dal-Mutg; Brahma Kumari Sudesh Dadi; Dr Jaswant Singh Neki of Bhai Vir Singh Sahitya Sadan; Ven. Rahul Bodhi of Bikku Sangha United Buddhist Mission, Sarvodya Maha Suddha Vihar, Mumbai; Maulana Wahiduddin of the Islamic Centre in New Delhi; and Yuvacharya Mahashraman and Sadhvi Pramukha Kanakprabha of Shwetambar Terapanth Community.

FOUNDATION FOR UNITY OF RELIGIONS AND ENLIGHTENED CITIZENSHIP (FUREC)

To pursue the philosophy of the Surat Declaration, FUREC was established on 15 June 2004. FUREC began with an advantage. It had, for the first time in recent history, leading representatives of all the living religions of the country. Fifteen spiritual leaders belonging to nine different religions came together on one platform to spread the message of harmony and peace. They sought to harness spiritual energy for social transformation: economic, societal and spiritual.

In the first year itself, FUREC held more than seventy meetings across the country where local representatives of different religions got together and expressed their solidarity and commitment to the cause. This was done in many ways. Functions were organized on important festivals of the different religions in which people from all the religions participated. Processions were taken out through the streets of the towns to send a message that all religious leaders desired betterment of humankind. Developmental activities in rural areas like building water tanks for schoolchildren or a compound wall for schools were undertaken with participation by local leaders and people of all faiths. Endal village in Tamil Nadu and villages near Adichunchanagiri in Karnataka and Ladnun in Rajasthan are some of the places where substantial healthcare, education and social activities were undertaken. Round table discussions were held in different parts of the country wherein the executive body met with the intelligentsia and a two-way communication was established. Also, students from all corners of India were addressed during these events.

In the years that followed, FUREC multiplied its activities. It launched an all-India essay competition in English that later became an annual feature and expanded to Kannada and Hindi. More than 30,000 students have taken part in it so far and seven books of compilation of the essays have been released.

FUREC conducted more than a thousand workshops in Delhi schools to develop understanding of peace and non-violence. To develop education and healthcare awareness, a project has been undertaken in Adichunchanagiri under the aegis of the Sri Sri Sri Balagangadharnatha Swamiji. The seer identified fourteen skills, and training workshops have been set up in more than eleven villages where youth are being trained regularly in vocations like carpentry, welding and tailoring. Swamiji has established a separate cadre of heath workers who go to the villages and help people, particularly women, to access medical health.

FUREC functions at three levels. At the level of the individual, it seeks to develop a common agenda for the development of an individual free of violence, so that we can have enlightened citizens. At the level of the society, it seeks to eradicate poverty through economic upliftment and harnessing the teachings of spirituality. At the collective level, it seeks to bring about better understanding between the different faiths and religions and amity between them. Given below is a conversation Acharyaji and I recently had:

Acharya: Kalam, I recall that we together launched a very important movement on 15 October 2003, which also happens to be your birthday. The occasion was graced by fifteen spiritual leaders and their teams at Surat. For the first time in our country, a structured action-oriented system was evolved, bringing together spiritual connectivity. Looking back, can you tell me what impact it has made amongst our people, particularly the youth.

Kalam: Acharyaji, the birth of FUREC led to many programmes, one of them being the the yearly essay competition for the children. Thousands of students participate, and we have released their work in the form of books on many occasions. These books are indeed the windows into the health of our families.

Acharya: Did the movement of righteousness among the youth emerge out of FUREC?

Kalam: There is an interesting episode. At Adichunchanagiri, a Class X student, Bhavani, asked me a question in front of a gathering of 54,000, consisting of students, teachers, religious leaders and parents. 'Mr. Kalam, I want to live in a corruption-free India, Can you please tell me, as a youth what should I do?' This led to the birth of the movement of righteousness. Daily, thousands of youths visit my website www.abdulkalam.com on this issue.

Acharya: Blessed are the nations whose children are awakened.

DIVINE SCIENCE

Scientists, philosophers and theologists and spiritual leaders have to eventually converge towards an understanding of what may be called divine science. These are spiritual, mystical, religious and theological truths of the contemporary world. The Divine Science would be a result of breakthroughs in understanding the fundamental basis of Reality such as quantum theory, relativity theory, chaos theory, general systems theory, string theory, and others. The magnitude of infinite possibilities within the human body and external cosmos is amazing. Divine Science has to transcend the certainty of strictly Newtonian clockwork notions to a new vision of a holistic and unified cosmos rooted in a non-local quantum reality that is fundamentally spiritual as opposed to material. It may also be described as intrinsically evolutionary and harmonious. The FUREC and institutions like Future Nalanda University can promote this doctrine.

Part 2

THE INDIVIDUAL, THE FAMILY AND THE NATION

4

Creating Healthy Individuals

> *Heaven lieth at the feet of mothers. God's pleasure is in a father's pleasure; and God's displeasure is in a father's displeasure. He who wisheth to enter Paradise at the best door must please his father and mother.*
>
> —Al-Quran

It is very human to act entirely upon intense but unconscious emotional considerations rather than on objective and conscious intellectual inference. For, as unrealized souls, we are not rational beings. We are only human beings, so our irrational emotions are natural.

In the Mahabharata, overwhelmed by despair and desiring to flee the battlefield, Arjuna begins his monologue to justify his wish to put down arms. So it is with all of us. Swamped by indefensible emotion, we vindicate ourselves with reason and logic. When our incongruent decisions and actions threaten our ego, we seek refuge in rationalization. While acting in defence of the ego, the intellect of man serves as an engine for sustaining illusion. Can this intellect be freed from ego to become a powerful instrument that facilitates higher human traits?

The Mahabharata dwells at length on this aspect. The arguments and logic of Arjuna are the rationalizations, the defence mechanism of the ego. Denial of Dhritarashtra's blindness, literal as well as figurative, is another defence mechanism. Confirmation bias is a tool that props up this mechanism. The mind always finds innumerable references from authorities as well as scriptures that confirm his rationalizations. An uncontrolled mind tends to give collaborative examples to further the dictates of the ego.

This false image or ego that we entertain about ourselves appears integral to both our material existence and our peace of mind. Yet the truth is that we are whatever our destiny commands us to be at that moment. Our false sense of identity and image imprison us and prevent us from responding to the call of God and Providence.

An individual is the smallest unit of society. Society is like the thread of a rosary on which individuals pass through like beads. In Bhagwad Gita, Lord Krishna says, 'Mayi sarwa-midam protam sutre mani-gana iva'—Everything rests upon Me, as pearls are strung on a thread.

To understand and evaluate society, we have to consider the individuals. 'Yat pinde tat brahmande'—What constitutes an individual element (pinda) comprises the cosmos (Brahamanda). This philosophical maxim is the needle of the compass that helps us understand society. Society is reflected in an individual. If the mirror in the form of an individual is clean, we can see in him the reflection of a healthy society.

What is an individual? The reflection on individuality leads to knowledge, sensation, feeling, experience, sensory consciousness, mental consciousness, dispositional consciousness, birth, death, and many similar individual attributes. Similarly, a reflection on society leads to relationship, mutuality, collaboration and dependence. However, the minds of men are confused today, and the very foundations of our civilization seem to be tottering. More and more people, particularly among the younger generation, are losing faith in existing institutions. The wise realize that a capitalist, industry-driven democracy is defeating the very purpose it is supposed to serve. Our democracy has not achieved unity of minds. The struggle of opposing ideas as witnessed in the country today involves social problems urgently demanding a solution. We are facing the crises of education and health, poverty and unemployment, terrorism, domestic violence, distressed family relations, etc. We have a democratically elected government, free media, free market economy, and yet we lack an integrated solution to our societal needs.

In our view, the individual is the true reality of life. A cosmos in himself, he does not exist for the government, nor for that abstraction called 'society,' or the 'nation,' which is only a collection of individuals. Man has always been, and necessarily is, the sole source and motive power of evolution and progress. Every civilization has gone through a process of struggle of the individual or groups of individuals against a structured governing system.

Man's greatest battles have been waged against man-made obstacles and artificial handicaps thrust upon him to paralyse his growth and development. Human thought has always been bound in by tradition and custom, and education has always been perverted to suit the interests of those in power. This constant conflict has been a common feature through the history of mankind.

How do we define individuality? Individuality may be described as the consciousness of an individual about who he is and how he lives. It is inherent in every human being and is a factor of growth. Governments and social institutions come and go, but individuality remains and persists. The very essence of individuality is its sense of dignity and independence. Governments tend to see individuality as impersonal and mechanistic but it is not so. The individual is not merely the result of heredity and environment, of cause and effect. He is a great deal more. He is the fountainhead of all life and all values. Yet he is not a part of this; he is a separate whole, ever growing and ever changing.

Individuality cannot be confused with the various ideas and concepts of Individualism, which are only masked attempts to repress and defeat the individual and his individuality. So-called Individualism is the social and economic laissez faire: the exploitation of the masses by some classes through legal trickery, spiritual debasement and systematic programming of the spirit into obedience. The straitjacketing of individuality can convert life into a degrading race for externals—acquisitions, social prestige, supremacy and power.

So does not life begin and end with the individual? In the words of Emma Goldman (1869–1940), 'The society is but the shadow of man, the shadow of his opaqueness, of his ignorance and fear.'

APHORISMS OF HEALTH

Hippocrates[1] wrote in 400 BC, 'Life is short, and Art long; the crisis fleeting; experience perilous, and decision difficult.' We know that humans are profoundly emotional beings, and unless we understand our emotions, we are very often powerless over our own actions, and therefore powerless over the world. We believe that by coming to know our powerful emotions, we can maximize peace and joy in our lives. We therefore made a decision to try and understand how our thinking and actions are often greatly determined by our past and present emotions.

We believe that only by taking a detailed emotional inventory of our anger, fear, distress, disgust and shame, and by assessing what we are really interested in and what really makes us happy, can we truly be able to change our actions. Which is why when we make the effort to express to others and ourselves the exact nature of our feelings, we gain some power over them. Those who are ready to accept the world and others as they are, are healthier than those who resist reality. Based on these experiences, we have developed certain aphorisms guided by which one can interact with others. The idea behind these aphorisms is that health is a multifaceted condition that includes the physical, the emotional, the spiritual, and more. All of them are inter-related and interdependent.

Freedom

The first aphorism of a healthy individual is freedom or independence, which essentially means an unfettered ability to choose. A person who is subjugated is plagued by emotional disorders or distress. How can such a person be physically and mentally sound? If an individual succumbs to the dictates of his senses and mind and indulges arbitrarily, he suffers from an absence of restraint (svachhandata). But if he analyses the dictates of his senses and mind and uses discretion, he experiences freedom (svatantrata).

Slavery doesn't mean mere bondage to others and a compulsion to comply with the orders of others. Slavery also means to give in to one's arbitrary impulses or primal drives. It amounts to a sort of depravity. A person enslaved by his impulses cannot be healthy.

Self-control

The second essential attribute of health is the power of self-control. The rashness of anger, arrogance, deceit, hypocrisy, greed, libido, fear and desire make the brain imbalanced.

A person with an imbalanced brain cannot be healthy. The human body is governed by the mind (mana). Mind is governed by emotions (bhava). Emotions are governed by the emotional heart (hridya). The emotional heart is different from the physiological heart, which is located in the chest, beneath the lungs, and is responsible for the circulation of blood. The emotional heart is in the brain. It gives rise to feelings. It can be identified with the hypothalamus, which is part of the limbic system. There is a centre in the middle of the posterior hypothalamus called the dorsomedial nucleus. It triggers anger. In the terminology of the Doctrine of Karma,[2] it is called the state of the soul caused by the rising of Karma (audayika bhava). The ventomedial nucleus, embedded in the hypothalamus, generally blocks anger. In Karmic terminology, it is called the state of the soul caused by the elimination or subsidence of the eight types of Karma (ksayopasamika bhava). Both the hypothalamus and cerebral cortex (mastiska-chhala) cause stimulation as well as regulation of emotions.

There are three degrees of stimulation, namely, intense, medium and slow. Intense inflammation of anger generates ailments like high blood pressure and heart disease. Emotions like arrogance, guilt, hypocrisy, greed and fear also cause various kinds of diseases. It is essential to restrain the intense type of stimulation for maintaining general health. In order to promote spiritual health, the medium and slow types of stimulation also need to be controlled. However, not all individuals may be able to exercise total control over the three types of stimulation.

Certain emotions are seen to be linked to particular ailments. Our friend Dr. M.A. Saleem says, 'Anger leads to high blood pressure. Tendency to protest irritates the bowels. Insults and humiliation lead to disorders of the digestive system. Intense lust leads to chest pain. Unjustifiable desires leads to skin disease. Mental suffocation leads to headache. Jealousy is linked to ulcers and too much ambition causes diabetes.'

The fundamental element of spiritual therapy is purity of emotions. The best medium to understand and explain human attitude and behaviour is the medium of emotions. There are five important facts to understand about this medium: (1) Hypothalamus is very sensitive to emotions and feelings; (2) The emotions continue to affect the body through the involuntary nervous system and the endocrine glands; (3) We have no control on the involuntary nervous system but it can be affected by emotions; (4) The waves of emotions are amenable to transformation by the subconscious mind; and (5) Treatment of disease is possible through transformation of emotions. With each emotion, certain subatomic material clusters are formed. Ominous emotions form inauspicious material clusters that weaken the mind and body. Good emotions, on the other hand, form positive material clusters that strengthen the immunity system of the body.

Fearlessness

The third aphorism of health is an environment free from fear. Modern man's mind is impulsive and unsteady and easily affected by circumstances, especially those that give rise to fear. Fear generates tremendous tension. Sudden fear may even cause a heart attack. There is an intimate relationship between freedom (svatantrata) and fearlessness (abhaya). Freedom makes man fearless and slavery instils fear. In fact, both freedom and fearlessness are two sides of the same coin; one without the other is impossible.

In Ayurveda,[3] three kinds of humours are indicated—vata (wind), pitta (bile) and kapha (phlegm). If all the three are in perfect balance, there is good health. An imbalance indicates a diseased state. Enthusiasm, inhalation and exhalation are all natural functions of vata. All activities in a living creature take place on account of vata; it is nothing but the prana of a living creature. It is due to vata that diseases are caused and it is due to vata again that diseases are cured. According to Ayurveda, fear impairs or damages the vata system. A frightened person has breathing disorder and is unable to work.

Although there are many sources of fear, the main source is the excessive accumulation of wealth. Wealth passes through three states—the state of earning, the state of preservation, and the state of destruction. Knowingly or unknowingly, a person's mind is always bothered by the security or otherwise of his wealth. Can an affluent person ever be free from fear? Attachment, acquisitiveness, fear and disease run in parallel to one another.

The first step for an aspirant of salvation is the renunciation of attachment. The words sthitprajna (equanimity) and vitaraga (free from attachment and aversion) represent a state where attachment, acquisitiveness and fear melt away. This truth, meant for those who desire salvation (mumuksu), is also meant for those who want to live a healthy life free from fear.

If the subtle reactions caused in the brain by fear are examined, we realize that they are not free from elements that cause diseases. The environment of fear is not created by external circumstances alone; internal circumstances play an equally significant role. Due to internal fears, a person may fall victim to a disease even in the absence of any external situation of fear.

Moderation

The fourth aphorism of good health is self-restraint. Human activity is an interplay of body, mind and speech. Sense organs are conjoined with the body. Ayurveda gives a twofold epistemology of disease: (1) Not to perform the activities of body, speech, mind and senses on account of laziness (ayoga); (2) Not to indulge in excessive activity of the body, speech, mind and senses (atiyoga). In the present age, excessive indulgence or abundance of unrestricted activity is causing a plethora of diseases known as lifestyle diseases, which affect both body and mind. Conquering the senses (jitendriya) and restraining the senses (indriya-samyam) are fundamental to good health. He who has pure and righteous emotions has control over his mind. His senses only perceive the respective qualities of objects without any sentiment of attachment or aversion towards them. Such a person can be said to have conquered the senses.

Acquisition of the qualities of objects that gratify the senses and the mind (vishayas) is a natural process of life. It is also natural to develop feelings of attachment or hatred, pleasure or displeasure towards the vishayas that are acquired. The feelings of love and hatred and of pleasure and displeasure always vary in intensity. One who knows the detrimental consequences of developing likes and dislikes for vishayas, does not allow liking to degenerate into attachment or dislike to degenerate into hatred. On the other hand, he who doesn't ponder the consequences of indulging in attachment or hatred is carried away by them and becomes a slave to these emotions. Such a state is hazardous to health.

Just as we need to put a comma or full stop in a sentence for clarity of meaning, we also need to apply a comma or full stop to our tendency of developing the feelings of pleasure or displeasure towards an object or idea. We can call this punctuation process an act of self-restraint. He who fails to put a comma or full stop to his tendency to indulge in worldly pleasures falls prey to an insatiable desire and this insatiability drives him to crime or makes him mentally ill.

It is evident from the history of medical science that medicines do not solve all problems of health, particularly those emanating from lifestyles as well as scarcity of amenities and hygiene. Poverty, starvation, disintegration of families, mental tension, and impulsive habits are very powerful factors in deciding health. The problem of starvation and poverty is economical and eventually political. The problem of disintegration of families is bound up with emotional problems. The problem of mental tension and impulsive surge is associated with the built-in consciousness.

The problem of poverty can be solved in a healthy economy and society. The problem of disintegration of families can be solved by a healthy social system and positive thoughts. The problem of mental tension and impulsive reactions can be solved by awakening the spiritual consciousness. In our view, only the integrated and holistic efforts of economists, political leaders, social reformers, medical experts, psychologists and spiritual practitioners can solve the problems of a healthy society. Such a concerted effort can lead to a society free from violence and crime.

Broadmindedness

The fifth aphorism of health is tolerance. Intolerance has been ever present in human history. It has triggered wars, fuelled religious persecution and violent ideological confrontations. Is it inherent in human nature? Is it insurmountable? Can tolerance be learned? How can democracies deal with intolerance without infringing on individual freedom? How can they foster individual codes of conduct without laws and without policing their citizens' behaviour? How can peaceful multiculturalism be achieved? There are many problems in the world, but perhaps the biggest is that of reconciling individuality with the demands of society. The foundation of a healthy society indeed lies in bringing about harmony among diverse needs, ideas, thoughts and interests. The vital element of harmony is tolerance.

Intolerance in a society is the sum total of the intolerance of its individual members. Bigotry, stereotyping, stigmatizing, insults and racial jokes are examples of individual expressions of intolerance to which some people are subjected daily. Intolerance breeds intolerance. It leaves its victims in pursuit of revenge. In order to fight intolerance, individuals should become aware of the link between their behaviour and the vicious cycle of mistrust and violence in society. Each one of us should begin by asking: Am I a tolerant person? Do I stereotype people? Do I reject those who are different from me? Do I blame my problems on them?

What is tolerance? Tolerance is respect, acceptance and appreciation of the rich diversity of our world's cultures, our forms of expression and ways of being human.[4] It is fostered by knowledge, openness, communication, and freedom of thought, conscience and belief. Tolerance is harmony in difference. Tolerance is a moral duty. Tolerance is the virtue that makes peace possible, and contributes to the replacement of the culture of war by a culture of peace.

Tolerance is, above all, an active attitude prompted by the recognition of universal human rights and fundamental freedoms of others. Tolerance is to be exercised not only by individuals but more so by social groups and governments. What is intolerance? Intolerance is everything that tolerance is not—it is narrow-mindedness, prejudice and fanaticism.

Education is the most effective means of preventing intolerance. The first step in 'tolerance education' should be to teach people what their shared rights and freedoms are, so that they may be respected, and to promote the will to protect those of others. Education for tolerance should be considered as an urgent imperative. It is necessary to promote systematic and rational tolerance teaching methods to address the cultural, social, economic, political and religious sources of intolerance.

Education policies and programmes should contribute to the development of understanding, solidarity and tolerance among individuals as well as among ethnic, social, cultural, religious and linguistic groups. Education for tolerance should also aim at countering influences that lead to fear and exclusion of others, and should help young people to develop capacities for independent judgment, critical thinking and ethical reasoning.

Balanced Nervous System

The sixth aphorism of health is a balanced nervous system. The human body has a set of systems to coordinate and regulate the body. The nervous system is one of these systems which acts as a communication network. The nervous system is made up of billions of individual cells called neurons, capable of carrying electrical messages or impulses at the rate of up to one hundred meters per second.

The Central Nervous System (CNS) is made up of the spinal cord and brain. The brain is the core. It receives, processes and responds to billions of signals twenty-four hours a day. The CNS combines with the Peripheral Nervous System (PNS) to control movement. The CNS controls balance, coordinates movement, and monitors and regulates what happens in the body.

The Autonomic Nervous System (ANS) is the unconscious part of the nervous system. It regulates the organs (the viscera) of our body, such as the heart, stomach and intestines. In most situations, we are unaware of the workings of the ANS because it functions in an involuntary, reflexive manner. For example, we do not notice when blood vessels change size or when our heart beats faster. The ANS is very important in two situations, namely, in emergencies that cause stress and require us to fight or take flight (through its sympathetic component), and in normal circumstances when we are required to rest and digest (through its parasympathetic component).

The PNS consists of sensory neurons running from stimulus receptors that inform the CNS of the stimuli. Motor neurons then run from the CNS to the muscles and glands—called effectors—that take necessary action.

For preservation of health, it is imperative that these nervous systems remain balanced. If the sympathetic component becomes overactive, it breeds an egoistic feeling. The overactive parasympathetic component breeds inferiority complex. Their imbalance gives rise to various mental illnesses. The knowledge of vital energy (pranas) is very relevant in this context. There are three pathways (nadis) through which vital energy flows: ida, pingla and sushumna.

The main function of ida is to provide rest, peace and orderliness of the mind. The function of pingla is to stimulate activity. The function of sushumna is to establish contact with the inner consciousness. For a regulated life, it is imperative that all three channels remain open and in equilibrium. Any imbalance in the pranic flow can cause a physical or mental disorder.

Biochemical Balance

Health depends primarily on two major factors: adequate nutrition and efficient elimination. Our well-being improves through correct nutrition, which leads to biochemical changes that promote emotional balance and lift the spirit.

Crass commercialization has taken a toll on nutrition. The mass marketing efforts by food conglomerates, whose main interest is profit, compounded by misinformation by conventional healthcare institutions and their affiliates, make it difficult to differentiate between life-giving, nutritious food and sub-standard, devitalized food. It's becoming more and more difficult to obtain clean, wholesome food as people have taken to processed and fortified food products in the belief that they are more nutritious. Such foods don't just have preservatives, additives, flavourings and colourings, they also have chemical pesticides and fertilizer residuals. Is it a wonder that degenerative diseases such as cancer, diabetes, arthritis and others are escalating proportionately? Is it a surprise that many of our children, particularly in urban areas, are diagnosed with attention deficit disorder (ADD/ADHD)[5] and other biochemical disturbances that are devastating their families, and ultimately, societies?

Instead of going to the core of the problem, mainly nutritional deficiency, we perpetuate and compound the situation by overmedicating our children. What are we doing to our children? What are we doing to ourselves as a species? How can we claim to nurture and protect our young while giving them food and water laced with chemicals? This is not what Nature intended. Why do we persist in destroying the very thing that nourishes and sustains us? How much longer can we delay the real solution?

We think we are untouched because some of us are fortunate enough to have eluded illness thus far. But with cancer striking one in five persons, heart disease taking more lives of people in their forties, countless people subsisting with crippling pain and deformity, what makes us the exception? We can no longer pretend that we are not aware. Regardless of what the disease is called, its root cause is still deficiency and toxicity. The typical conventional methods of cut (surgery), burn (radiation), and poison (medication) have little effect as they do not address these issues. What if some are able to buy a little more time at the expense of quality of life?

How does it matter one way or the other?

Fortunately, Nature is forgiving and our bodies are wonderfully and powerfully created. Unless it has reached a point of no return, the body is capable of regeneration, if given the opportunity. The only sure way of achieving this is by going back to Nature, providing our body with proper nutrients while efficiently eliminating built-up toxins and debris.

The seventh aphorism of health is therefore biochemical balance. Emotional disorder is another reason for biochemical imbalance. When the emotions are stimulated intensely, biochemical secretions become unbalanced, creating several physical disorders. It will not be inappropriate to say that our health mostly depends on our ability to think positively and refine our emotions. There are three glands mainly responsible for maintaining health—pituitary, adrenal and gonads. Their balanced secretions maintain homeostasis in the body and an imbalanced secretion causes disorder in the body, mind and emotions.

There is a life-sustaining force in every human being. In philosophical language, it is called alimentary bio-potential (ahara paryapti). In medical science, it is called metabolism. The alimentary bio-potential involves three actions, namely, taking in (grahana); transformation (parinamana); and excretion or emptying the bowels (utsarjana).

Besides the type of food, the quantity of food we take is also very important. If a person avoids taking food which is in excess of his requirement, he can save himself from many ailments. The primary logic of fasting is restraining the quantity of food (unodari) taken. Ayurveda gives the guideline that one should eat only half of what one's hunger dictates. The formula of intake is given as half space for food, one-quarter space for water and one-quarter space for gases. One of the main causes of negative thoughts is neglect of the bowels. During fasting, when the digestive fire of the stomach does not have food to burn, it starts consuming toxins which would have led to ailments. By burning these toxins, fasting can be said to delay the ageing process.

Right Conduct

The eighth aphorism of health is ethical conduct (charitra). According to Plato, good is an essential element of Reality. Evil does not exist in itself but is, rather, an imperfect reflection of the Real, which is good. According to Plato, human virtue lies in the fitness of a person to perform his proper function in the world. The human soul has three elements—intellect, will and emotion. Each possesses a specific virtue in the good person and performs a specific role. The virtue of intellect is wisdom or knowledge of life; that of will is courage and the capacity to act; that of emotion is temperance or self-control. The ultimate virtue—justice—is the harmonious relation of all the elements, each fulfilling its appropriate task and keeping its proper place. Plato maintained that the intellect is sovereign, that the will is second to the intellect, and that the emotion is subject to both. The just person, whose life is ordered in this way, is therefore a good person.

German philosopher George Wilhelm Friedrich Hegel (1770–1831) placed ethics in a social context. According to Hegel, to be ethical is to fulfil one's duty to the best of one's ability. Hegel claimed that a man's reason and desires can be bridged by the recognition on the part of each person that he or she is part of a community. Since the individual is shaped by the community in which he lives, the community fosters those desires in him that benefit the community the most. Therefore, the individual should not pursue interests that contradict the interests of the community. Hegel spoke of three major circles in which a person should fulfil his or her duties—the family, the civic community, and the state. The state is the highest expression of both the spirit of the world and the individual. The right conduct of the individual would then be to pursue the common purpose of the state.

Ayurveda termed ethical conduct as a sort of medicine (rasayana). A person develops love for an object he likes and hatred for one he dislikes. Even when he gets the object which is dear to him, it only adds fuel to his desire for more. The mentally insatiate person takes to crime. Theft, deception, falsehood, treachery and greed ruin a person's conduct. A person who is not gratified or satiated indulges in forbidden action. He takes recourse to lying in order to preserve the object he is infatuated with. Before he tells a lie, he draws a net of guileful tactics, which results in tension. While lying, he experiences an inner tension. And after he has lied, he remains under tension to hide it. A vicious circle of tension is thus created.

Lies can be categorized in many different ways, but a widely held view is that there are four types of lies: Pro-social—lying to help someone else; Self-enhancement—lying to make yourself look better while not hurting another; Selfish—lying to personally benefit at the expense of another; and Anti-social—lying to deliberately damage another. Psychologists have concluded that there are four signs of someone lying: Avoidance of eye contact—usually someone makes eye contact at least half the time they are talking to you. If you notice them avoiding eye contact or looking down during a specific part of a conversation, they may well be lying; Change of voice—a variation in pitch of voice or rate of speech can be a sign of lying. People also use irrelevant words and sounds while lying; Body language—turning your body away, covering your face or mouth, a lot of fidgeting of hands or legs can indicate deception. Contradicting yourself

—a person making statements that just don't hold together indicates that he is lying.

Just Society

The ninth and last aphorism is healthy economics. Wealth is one of the most important needs of a person's life. So much so that money should be added to the list of air, light and heat, bread, water, clothing, house, medicines, for each of these things comes out of money. A society that is dominated by wealth as well as the one that suffers from its scarcity are both sick. How can individuals living in a sick society remain healthy? Those who live a life of deprivation suffer from worrying about bread. The Sanskrit words for worry (chinta) and funeral pyre (chita) are very similar. There is a difference of just one dot. Just as on a funeral pyre a dead body is burnt, in the same way worry consumes a person during his life. A person suffering from penury neither gets nourishment nor the essential minimum needs. Hence, the needy cannot be deemed as physically, mentally or emotionally healthy. At the other end, rich people suffer because of overconsumption of material objects. They lack satisfaction because they have too much of everything. Both rich and poor can be found using drugs and alcohol. A needy person takes to them to lessen his anxiety and pain. The rich take to them to lessen their perennial anxiety over the safety of their wealth.

Despite all the progress made by humanity, economic disparity has not been reduced. Rather, it has increased. More than 50 per cent of workers all over the world live on less than $2 a day. In India, 220 million people live below the poverty line. Globalization is taking away the livelihood of people engaged in making small articles of domestic use. Cottage and small-scale industries cannot compete with big corporations. We cannot solve the problem created by capitalism through a capitalistic system. The solution lies only in awakening man's spiritual consciousness and instilling in him an awareness of renunciation and self-restraint. As an African proverb says, 'Two hundred cattle are under one stick, but two hundred human beings are under two hundred sticks.'

THE ACT OF TRANSFORMATION

Is it not a matter of great surprise that though we have sown a seed and a tree has grown, it has borne no fruit? The seed of the knowledge that we sow does grow to be a big tree, but it is bereft of fruit. The fruit of knowledge is conduct. In the human brain, there is a specialized region where knowledge is processed and another region where conduct is cultivated.

While freedom of the self is very important to good health, mindfulness about the value of another's freedom is equally important. To know that all humans are equal and all souls are equal is theoretical knowledge. To translate it into action, the practice of conduct (aachaara) is required. A little contemplation would tell us: 'As I don't like suffering, others too would not like it. Just as I am free to amass means of comfort, others are also free to do so. My freedom should not usurp the freedom of others. I should take care that I don't become an impediment in the way of others trying to collect means of comfort.' This sort of ethical conduct is an empirical aspect of the principle of equality. If we enter the periphery of a still subtler world, we will realize how we create obstacles in the path of others' freedom. Before creating such hurdles, we should ponder the fact that we cannot harm others without harming ourselves. We cannot take away others' freedom without our own freedom being taken away.

Theoretical doctrine and philosophy, no doubt, have their due importance. But they cannot help us attain the state wherein real transformation of our inner consciousness takes place. This requires a practical approach. Whatever man listens to and reads, affects only his conscious mind. It does not lead to his transformation. For transformation to happen, a person has to delve into the layers of the subconscious mind. Memory, feeling and emotion are all stored in the subconscious mind. Transformation is possible only when ideas and thoughts reach that level. In essence, we can say that books can take a person to the elementary stage of transformation; they cannot go beyond that. In order to take thoughts to the periphery of our subconscious mind, we need to deepen the concentration of the meditating mind to a state where thoughts disappear. A wilful and sustained effort is essential for this transformation.

AN ACT OF VOLITION

In the Upanishads, three steps of inner transformation are described. These are learning (sravana), practice (manana), and realization (nididhyasana). The Agamas mention five steps for the process of inner transformation: learning (sravana); knowledge (jnana); discernment or elucidation of right and wrong (vijnan viveka); abandonment of what is wrong (pratyakhyana); and self-restraint (sanyama). In our view, the best means to bring about a change in the attitudinal tendencies of human beings are two-fold, namely education (shiksha) and righteousness (dharma).

Why is it that even educated people remain unchanged, emotionally crude and bereft of compassion? Why do ethical values elude them? Why are even those studying Dharma insensitive and unaware? This has led to a situation where both Dharma and education are being doubted for their ability to transform human nature. The reason is that both these fields can bring about only an incomplete transformation. Through education, students are told what is right and what is wrong, but they are not trained to abandon the wrong. In the field of Dharma too a similar lacuna exists. Religious persons are not taught how to control their senses and mind. They are only taught to believe that they can reach their goal by observing rites and rituals. The pressing need of the present day is to effect the process of transformation.

The process of transformation is also fraught with a conflicting situation which we don't want to hide. Man has some inborn tendencies, of which the tendency to struggle, search for food and indulge in sex are the most dominating. Briefly, there are two basic passions—attachment and hatred. And of these two, the more vital one is attachment. The emotion on which attachment depends is called priyata. Emotions leave a deep impact on an individual's ethical conduct and behaviour. The intensity of the vibrations of attachment and hatred vary from man to man, because of which we see the variance in the ethical conduct and behaviour of individuals.

On account of the diverse degrees of basic passions, it is neither possible to make human beings behave uniformly nor cast all humans in the same mould. Rather, we should focus on controlling the development of these tendencies. It is a myth that human beings do not want to change or that they do not have the competence to change. In society, we may find about 10 per cent people with underdeveloped brains, another 10 per cent with partially developed brains, and another 10 per cent who are overwhelmed by intense basic passions. If we leave these 30 per cent, we still have the 70 per cent who have the desire to change.

YOGA

Yoga (from Sanskrit yuj, meaning yoke)[6] is an ancient family of spiritual practices. Yoga practices share a common goal—

samadhi, the complete integration of the Self with God. Traditionally, yoga consists of eight fundamental paths (ashtamargas): Karma yoga, Bhakti yoga, Jnana yoga, Hatha yoga, Purna yoga, Tantra yoga, Maha yoga and Ashtanga or Raja yoga. Yoga entails mastery over the body, mind, and emotional self, and transcendence of desire.

Patanjali's text sets forth eight parts of yoga practice (ashtanga yoga), namely: (1) Yama (the five abstentions)—violence, lying, theft, sex, and possessions; (2) Niyama (the five observances)—purity, contentment, austerities, study, and surrender to God; (3) Asana (seat)—originally referring mainly to seated positions; (4) Pranayama—control of prana or vital breath; (5) Pratyahara (abstraction)—that by which the senses do not come into contact with their objects and, as it were, follow the nature of the mind; (6) Dharana (concentration)—fixing attention on a single object; (7) Dhyana (meditation); and (8) Samadhi—superconscious state or trance. The two principles of physical exercise of postures (asanas) and the exercise of breathing (pranayam), and the first two principles of Jain spiritual practice, namely, fasting and physical postures, offer a very effective yoga system.

Asanas help us to achieve physical health, but they also bring about a change in a person's attitude. Any physical activity, in general, causes production of lactic acid in the system which in turn causes tension. Its cure lies in suspension of activity through kayotsarga. It comprises relaxation of the body together with awareness of every limb and renunciation of the feeling of attachment towards one's body. Shavasana (a posture in which a person simulates a corpse) of Hatha yoga is a good exercise for relaxation.

Hatha yoga classifies the seven benefits of practising asanas: (1) prevention of obesity; (2) cheerfulness on one's face; (3) clarity and sweetness of voice; (4) health; (5) virility;

(6) increased appetite; and (7) clean blood vessels, bronchi, bowels, etc.

Correspondingly, there are seven basic ingredients of good health: (1) flexibility of spinal column; (2) efficiency of lungs; (3) efficiency of heart; (4) efficiency of kidneys; (5) efficiency of liver, spleen and digestive system; (6) balanced hormonal secretions; and (7) strong nervous system.

Pranayam

The process of breathing is not only a vital means of sustaining life but is also the foundation of wholesome development. In a scientific manner, Patanjali proceeds from the external sheath of man and slowly proceeds to the subtler sheaths. Breath and mind are closely interdependent and interpenetrating. Control of breath means the cessation of the outgoing and ingoing movements of breath. Breath is the gross representative of the subtle, vital force inside the body. Just as by stopping of the key of a timepiece you do not allow it to move and the cog wheels, and finally the hair-spring, come to a standstill, by controlling the force which sets into motion the mind, we can stop the motion of the mind. It is Prana that makes the mind move. If Prana is stopped, the mind cannot move and a state of stillness (Manonasha) ensues.

Breathing comprises inhaling (puraka), exhaling (rechaka), and retaining the breath (kumbhaka). Correct breathing is healthy. In normal conditions, the average rate of breathing is 15-20 breaths per minute. It means breathing in for two seconds and breathing out for two seconds. But the number of breaths can escalate to sixty when the mind is agitated, which is highly detrimental to health. Through proper practice, one can bring down the breathing rate to a level that is beneficial for health.

At the heart of breathing exercises is the retention of breath (kumbhaka). The extended kumbhaka moments practised after inhalation give us an opportunity to assimilate oxygen and the vital force acquired through inhalation. Kumbhaka practised after exhalation facilitates expulsion of carbon dioxide efficiently. The general exercise of pranayam stipulates four seconds of inhaling, sixteen seconds of retention, and eight seconds of exhaling. At this point, we would like to discuss another prayer system in our society.

THE NAMAZ

We discussed the various prayer modes in an integrated way and their effect on body, mind and soul. Islam prescribes the conduct of namaz five times daily by every individual. The prescribed timings for namaz are: Fajr (morning immediately after sun rise), Zohar (noon between 1 and 2 pm), Asr (afternoon between 4 and 5 pm), Magrib (evening between 6 and 7 pm) and Isha (night from 9 pm onward). The namaz timings are prescribed in such a way that it does not affect the normal working hours of any person. The total duration of namaz extends between ten to twenty minutes at any one time. During namaz, the individual takes six physical positions for each part of the prayer. The prayer has a minimum of two parts and a maximum of four. In each pose, the individual recites a specific Quranic verse in praise of Allah. In the first pose, he recites Alfatiha, the first Sura, which means 'Praise be to Allah, the Lord of all creatures, the most gracious and most merciful, it is thee from whom we seek benevolence, guide us to the right path, the path of those to whom you have been merciful and not the path of those who are subjected to your wrath.' In the last pose, the individual's face touches the earth. This part is called Sijda, and the namazee says: 'Allah is great and I submit before him.' In this pose, the individual realizes the equality of every person irrespective of his worldly position and inculcates in himself the highest order of humility. I have seen my father, mother, brothers, sisters performing namaz five times a day. When I ask myself, how this practice has contributed to human development, I realize that a mind which prays is close to God every hour and in every action, which enables the person to be stress free. The namaz has been the binding fibre of our joint family. Humility automatically enters a praying heart. The namaz gives us a direct communion with Allah through purity of heart and total submission to Him. Prophet Hazrat Mohammad once said this to signify the importance of namaz, 'If there was a river at the door of your house and you bathed in it five times every day, would you say that any dirt would be left on you? Obviously, no dirt will be left on you'. A companion of the Prophet once asked him which deed was loved most by Allah. He said, 'Namaz which is performed at its time'.

CONTENTMENT

Only that person can be healthy who feels happiness, and happiness can only be felt by the person who has peace of mind. Fulfilment of basic needs, peace and happiness are the three things desired by man. These can be prioritized. To regulate the journey of life, fulfilling basic needs are a priority. Happiness is a priority for the agreeable feelings it generates. And comforts cannot give happiness to a person unless he has peace.

Rather than seek the gratification of desires, the Indian ethos espouses its antithesis—contentment—as the source of happiness. Contentment in this context refers to a state of mind in which the potential psychic energy, known as libido in Western psychology, is transformed into a serene mental quality, rather than actualized as a desire that needs to be gratified or repressed.

A craving for fame and wealth often results in moral depravity, and in many cases personal destruction. The greatest of woes comes from not knowing contentment; the greatest of faults comes from craving for gains. The nature of humanity and, for that matter, of all creatures, was to live in a simple way, partaking no more than what was needed to maintain the healthy growth of the organism. Beyond that limit were selfish craving and extravagance. A sage is free from excessive pursuit, enjoyment and expectation. A sage is not the product of moral cultivation but simply someone who lives according to his authentic nature. Alienation from this life of simplicity is the root cause of all human problems.

What are the implications of contentedness for modern people? First of all, one may raise the point that, unlike animals, human needs extend far beyond the physiological realm to cover psychological, emotional and spiritual needs. Even physiological needs change as civilization progresses. For example, several decades ago, people were content with riding a bicycle, but today driving a car has become a necessity for many of them.

The biggest folly of our times is that the young have been presented with a plethora of objects. The youth are not taught that achieving peace is impossible without limiting the demands of the senses and the mind. Since childhood, we see and hear things which indirectly endorse an attachment to worldly possessions. The infatuation of the young with worldly pleasures grows so strong that it becomes virtually impossible for them to reject the demands of the senses and the mind. The attitude of indifference to worldly pleasures (vairagya) has become an alien concept.

Both electronic and print media play a dominant role in fanning human passions. The main aim of the media is to disseminate news, and to an extent entertain, but it has gone beyond its limits by relentlessly showing scenes or events that intensify desire. How can we think that the society and the individual will be free from crimes if the youth are not able to spare a few moments to assess the significance of non-attachment (vairagya), while they have all the time to imbibe the idea of attachment to pleasures (raga)? Economic temptation is at the root of crass commercialization. Corporations want to earn unlimited wealth by cashing in on the human weakness of desire. Attachment to sensual pleasure is a human weakness. The media knowingly or unknowingly nurtures this weakness. We cannot turn a blind eye to the fact that in the name of religion, some people collect money and indulge in physical comforts. A new alliance between wealth and Dharma is emerging. Who will save the boat from the boatman who is bent upon sinking it?

There are two fundamental entities on this planet—sentient and non-sentient, or, in other words, soul and matter. We realize that the interest of people in spiritual knowledge is diminishing. They are now inclined more towards materialistic things. The reason is the absence of an antithesis. The antithesis of materialistic inclination is contentment (santosha). It is the upsurge of interest in materialistic objects that is responsible for the accumulation of wealth and consumer goods and intensification of a hedonistic outlook. On the other hand, the directions one receives from within are: forsaking wealth, restricting consumption and living a life of austerity.

The situation is rather grave. In the visible world, it is the matter which governs and hence plays the role of the party in government pushing soul into the opposition. The irony is that matter is non-sentient. It is neither able to think nor speak nor feel. And the effects of giving this attribute precedence can be seen everywhere. The air and water bodies are polluted. The excessive particulate matter of automobile and industrial exhaust in the air is giving rise to respiratory disorders and cancer of the lungs. Excessive use of chemical fertilizers is making soils infertile and polluting ground water. Climates are changing, leading not only to unpredictable weather but also to newer varieties of microbes that cause unheard of diseases.

SPIRITUAL TRAINING

A person is propelled to act on account of two sources of inspiration—individual and social. The individual source of inspiration stems from man's innate primal drives or propensities. The social source of inspiration owes its origin to social doctrines. After studying several political systems, it is not difficult to conclude that the individual source of inspiration is stronger than the social one. In order to bring about the desired attitudinal change, spiritual training becomes inevitable.

The cornerstones of such training could be: (1) I am a sentient being and material objects are non-sentient; (2) Material objects are only for my use, they don't belong to me; (3) Wealth may be essential and useful for the sustenance of my life. However, if I amass more than I need, it will spoil my health, create a cycle of social problems and give rise to violence by creating disparity among people; and (4) I will give up self-indulgence and practise non-possessiveness and self-discipline.

An important principle of the social and economic system is found in the aphorism 'parasparopagraho jivanam'—mutual assistance for all beings. It is a principle of social ethic. If this ethic is developed in the socio-economic system, there cannot be such a big gap between the rich and the poor. The problem of poverty can be solved only through moral development of the society.

CONTROLLING NEGATIVE ATTITUDES

One may not believe in Karma but the existence of attitude, feeling or emotion (bhava) cannot be denied. Negative feelings are definitely an obstacle in the attainment of good health. Sometimes, we cannot prevent being in their grip. Arousal of negative thoughts in our minds is a stark reality.

Why does this happen? If we try to seek an answer to this question in the imbalance of biochemical secretions, it will give rise to another question—why is this imbalance in biochemical secretions caused? If we try to seek the answer in the environment, it would lead to another question—why does this imbalance not occur in all individuals living in the same environment? Even in the principle of environment and heredity, we don't get a complete answer. The environment can be instrumental in the imbalance of biochemical substances, but it cannot be the root cause. The root cause is the flow of an individual's emotions (bhava). But this too doesn't put an end to the question.

Why does the negative current of emotions occur? Its root cause can be sought in delusion (moha). Delusion is related to the deepest level of consciousness. In every individual, there arise vibrations of delusion, which create a flow of bhava. The person whose delusion becomes weak is emancipated from reactions and his flow of bhava also becomes positive. The person whose delusion is intense carries with him a negative current of bhava.

Delusion is a type of psycho-physical structure (Karma). Delusion is marked by certainty, incorrigibility, and impossibility or falsity of content. The main cause of the negative flow of emotions is unrestrained desires or cravings. Desire, fulfilment and satiety are the three valleys or passages through which man's life keeps flowing. Desire is a characteristic of a living being and its fulfilment gives rise to temporary satisfaction. Man experiences a feeling of appeasement but only for a while. In a world where wealth and objects are important, desire continues to stretch like a rubber band. As the demand increases, the problem of supply gets complicated. The panacea to this malady lies in contentment (santosha). The view of contentment as a sop is erroneous. Contentment is indeed the highest form of bliss.

DEFEATING DISPARITY

The two questions—How far? How long?—have a special significance but these have been belittled. That is why the concept of development is also being totally misinterpreted. The human propensity for earning money by felling trees is the result of ignoring the question 'How long?'

Affluence and prosperity have become the measuring rods of development. Without discarding these measures, Nature cannot remain healthy, and without a healthy environment, how can an individual hope to be healthy? The concept of development formulated on the basis of mere physical and economic growth needs to be recast, taking into consideration the concept of complete health.

Ayurveda has a very well articulated criteria of complete health. A healthy person is one who has the following: (1) spiritual blissfulness; (2) gracious sense organs; (3) gracious mind; (4) cheerful sleeping and waking states; (5) wholesome food; (6) salutary movements and manners; (7) ability to act after a critical examination; (8) detachment towards sensual passions; (9) balance in every situation; (10) truthfulness; and (11) forgiveness.

It is imperative that we develop a new outlook towards health for which mental equipoise is as essential as a balanced and nourishing diet, if not more. At a deeper level, complete health is intimately connected with education. Though health education is included in curricula, character building, moral values and health education are still viewed in isolation. An integration of all three is needed to develop a holistic outlook towards health.

A society can be regarded as healthy only when its citizens have high operational efficiency. Only that society makes progress whose citizens are rich in thought. The strength of a society lies in the organization of its members. Negative emotions like anger, arrogance, greed, jealousy and fear not only affect both physical and mental health but also sap the strength of society's organization. They shatter the very building blocks of unity.

From the grosser point of view, the three types of health are arranged in the following order of precedence: (1) physical health; (2) mental health; and (3) emotional health. But viewed from a subtle angle, this order is reversed to: (1) emotional health; (2) mental health; and (3) physical health. The imbalance between intellectual and emotional development is a problem that gives rise to many other problems. We ought to pay more attention to emotional development than to intellectual development. Even human rights are not secured in the absence of emotional development.

There are two kinds of tension—external and internal. The external tension originates in adverse conditions of stress. It disappears when there is a change in the circumstances. The causes of internal tension arise from within the self. Suppose a person abuses someone. After some time, the person who is abused calms down and the tension vanishes. However, the feelings of animosity caused by the abusive words stays within him. In spiritual parlance, it is called salya. It is like a thorn or a splinter which is stuck inside the body. The salya remains eternally in the inner world of bhava and continues to eat into the individual's health. To remove salya, the spiritual seekers have presented the options of forgiveness and friendliness.

To forgive and ask for forgiveness is an application of tolerance to be exercised by both parties involved in a conflict. It puts an end to the tension on both sides. It also mitigates bodily processes that weaken the immunity system.[7] People tend to handle Dharma very superficially. That is why Dharma is not benefitting people as it should. The philosophical foundation of Dharma is ultimately the purification of the soul. Emotional intelligence (bhava buddhi) constitutes the foundation of its applied form. It is also the foundation of health. Indeed the four pillars of health are: (1) friendliness; (2) a happy disposition that welcomes others' excellence without malice (pramoda-bhavana); (3) compassion; and (4) equanimity.

In politics, there is a maxim—no one is a foe or friend. If a person does not oppose the fulfilment of our selfishness, he is our friend; otherwise he is our foe. Political friendship is indeed a concord which is born out of selfishness and fear. Spiritual friendship is not like political friendship. It does not exist for any particular person. It is indeed a manifestation of one's own consciousness in the form of a positive feeling or attitude towards all. If there is friendliness, it is not for some but for all. It purges the subtle tension caused by selfishness and fear, thereby protecting and ensuring our health. Pramoda bhava arises from the pleasure one experiences on seeing the good fortune of others without any feeling of malice or jealousy. Jealousy is the antithesis of pramoda bhava. It is an emotional malice that leads to other diseases. However, it can come only in the absence of pramoda bhava.

The disposition of compassion is fundamentally based on the spiritual doctrine of the reality of soul. All souls are equal and undergo similar experiences of happiness and unhappiness. If we follow this principle, how can we create suffering for anyone else? That is the philosophical basis of the theory of compassion. It gets a practical form through control over various emotional impulses. The frenzied state of mind makes a person sick and eventually makes the society sick. It will be futile to expound the concept of holistic health by excluding from our consideration these two phenomena, namely, frenzy of the mind and subsidence of passions.

It is impossible to over-emphasize the point that the key to the process of induction, as used either in science or in our ordinary life, is to be found in the right understanding of the immediate occasion of knowledge in its full concreteness. Just as the minute living beings in a drop of water become visible only through a microscope, so too the exceedingly short-lived processes in the world of mind become cognizable only with the help of the instrument of mental scrutiny. A bias for a chosen few impedes the basic state of mind that is the soil of good health. It is important to capture and understand even momentary feelings of dislike or attachment.

English author Jerome K. Jerome (1859–1927) wrote in *Three Men in a Boat*: 'A family system is your boat in the river of life. It is a complete system in itself. As such, it is not possible that one member of the system can change without causing a ripple effect of change throughout the family system. The key elements of a family system are its members + beliefs + roles + rules + assets + limitations + goals + boundaries + subsystems (for example, siblings) + environment, a larger system of systems, or metasystem (for example, community).' In the next chapter, we will try to understand these elements and how their interaction can help family members to assess the nurturing role of the family.

Having met and interacted with youth and families, we discuss at this point the important elements that can remove the urge in young minds for acquiring wealth through wrong means and that can cultivate in them the yearning for a higher goal. Above all, we stress the ability to enjoy the success of others, which is indeed the highest order of emotional intelligence. Here, we recommend to all the educational institutions in the nation to include in the curriculum the following oath for all students up to the age of seventeen.

An Oath of Emotional Intelligence by the Youth

- I realize I have to set a goal in my life. To achieve the goal, I will acquire the knowledge, I will work hard, and when the problem occurs, I have to defeat the problem and succeed.
- As a youth of my nation, I will work and work with courage to achieve success in all my tasks and enjoy the success of others.
- I shall always keep myself, my home, my surroundings, neighbourhood and environment clean and tidy.
- I realize righteousness in the heart leads to beauty in the character, beauty in the character brings harmony in the home, harmony in the home leads to order in the nation and order in the nation leads to peace in the world.

If imbibed from a young age, this oath will help the growth of a righteous mind in the youth, steer them towards a purposeful life, and remove all stresses, thereby building future citizens with healthy minds and bodies.

5

The Birth of a Beautiful Home

We have made thee neither of heaven nor of earth, neither mortal nor immortal, so that with freedom of choice and with honour, as though the maker and moulder of thyself, thou mayest fashion thyself in whatever shape thou prefer.

—Giovanni Pico della Mirandola (1486)

THE INSTITUTION OF FAMILY

The home should be the happiest place we can ever know on earth, and a place that is a constant source of strength and inspiration. In it we have the closest and dearest relationships, which sustain us all our lives. But to create and preserve the happiness of the home requires certain qualities and attitudes.

The family is an institution of love, care, compassion and kindness. It brings progress, prosperity, peace and tranquillity in the society. It nurtures values and makes human beings civilized. A family comes into existence by the coming together of a man and a woman in marriage and their union creates a new family and a new generation. This family produces the tie of kinship and community, which develops into a large society. The family is the institution through which one generation prepares another for the service of human civilization. Members of this institution desire that those who replace them should be better than themselves. Parents want to see their children happier, healthier, more educated, and better human beings than their own selves. All religions place great emphasis on the family and family values.

As societies have shifted economically from agriculture to industry, extended families have largely given way to nuclear families. Family values, also, do not remain fixed and rigid; they change in response to economic, political and cultural developments. They vary from country to country, and even among different households.

Before the twentieth century, for example, in most places and at most times, the idea of a married woman seeking status and recognition independent of her husband would have constituted a breach of family values. Many societies expected women to focus exclusively on household duties. Indeed the family is a sort of societal laboratory. Both research and experiments are carried out here.

While family values remain a rather vague concept, sociologists usually understand the term to include a combination of at least four principles: (1) support for marriage as a lasting bond between one man and one woman; (2) family organization that has the husband as the head of the household and the wife primarily as homemaker; (3) parental responsibility for and control over children's education and discipline; (4) responsibility of aged parents and interaction with other relatives. While in a typical Indian family none of the four principles is violated outright, the compliance is no more natural and voluntary. There is a lot of underlying stress.

The crux of the institution of family is the blossoming of oneness in diversity. If there are ten members in a family, they will have their ten different modes of thinking and varying styles of working. Their emotions and emotional intensities may also be of various types. A family is all about living amicably in such a diverse environment and coexisting peacefully. We are happy with who we are. We respect others by accepting their race, religion, culture, opinions, hobbies or other interests as valuable to them. As we develop and express our various talents, we enrich each other's lives. Variety brings connectivity to the family.

An important principle of identity or oneness is love. It may be illustrated by a tree having many fruits. One of the fruits of the tree of love is humility and another is gratitude. These two fruits are the reverential gifts of the younger members of the family to the elders. Another fruit of the tree is affection. This is a gift that the elders in the family give to the younger ones. It is only in a family where the younger members have a deep feeling of humility and gratitude towards the older members that the aged get honour and respect. In such an environment of mutual humility, gratitude and affection, a person lives a life of joy. On the other hand, life becomes a burden in a family bereft of these values, and ultimately the sweetness of life evaporates.

The seed of a family is the feeling of mineness (mamatva). Without it, a family does not come into existence, or even if it does, it doesn't last long. We all belong to a family. Our family bonds gives us our identity, a way to recognize ourselves with a culture and heritage of our own. We support each other, depend on each other, respect each other and comfort each other. We are also members of larger families—our community, the human family, and the family of life on Earth. We accept the responsibilities of being a part of these families, only receiving what we need so that others may have their share, and helping to strengthen the family through our service.

Mamatva is a psychic instinct,[1] linked to its opposite, the feeling of self-assertion. Everyone loves freedom. Even a child likes freedom, leave alone the grownups. If either the feeling of self-assertion becomes unlimited or the chain of dependence too long, we cannot create a healthy family. In order to get rid of the feeling of self-assertion or the tendency of dependence, one has to make oneself free from mamatva. The feeling of self-assertion should not be allowed to become limitless.

The twin aphorisms of freedom and mamatva are: (1) The feeling of self-assertion should not take the form of unrestrained freedom; (2) Respect others' freedom. The human tendency to enslave others is linked to a feeling of self-assertion and the feeling of self-assertion is linked to mamatva. The solution to this complicated problem is relinquishing the feeling of mamatva or possessiveness, or at least placing a limit on it. A healthy person is one who considers both mamatva and the relinquishment of mamatva from a relative standpoint.

The first step of our action plan is to build a healthy individual and the next step is to build a healthy family and a beautiful home using healthy individuals as its building blocks. Each person thinks differently and has diverse interests. Conciliation and coordination among different members of a family is indeed a tough task. The individual is not alone in reality. He carries within him a family of myriad ideas and thoughts. Ideas too never remain uniform but change constantly.

THE PHILOSOPHY OF ANEKANTA

The family is a chain of relationships. Each link has its own significance. The two fundamental factors that create the chain are emotion and thought.

The pattern of surging emotions and thoughts in each individual undergoes a continuous change, which makes it difficult to keep intact the union of two persons. The 'all or none' approach has brought us to the brink of total annihilation; hence the concept that there is no single absolute interpretation of 'truth' and that a non-absolutist approach in thought, word and deed is the only way before us. Believing in pluralism—the existence of many perceptions about the same reality—and being open to discussions and arguments about different viewpoints provides a strong ground to hold different people together without conflict. Only a person with awareness about the validity of multiple views and opinions can accept others without grudge and remorse. Surely, a shared vision and an open attitude is needed to make familial or social life healthy and beautiful. The application of the philosophy of non-absolutism can fulfil this need.

Autonomy

The first principle of the philosophy of non-absolutism is freedom. Here, freedom does not mean merely a nation's independence or political freedom, but the autonomy of upholding one's choices while being intimately connected with every individual and without violating interpersonal relations. If you give value to your own freedom as well as that of others, then you already possess a building block of the vast mansion that is a happy family.

Know that every individual likes freedom. If you like freedom, can you not relinquish the mentality of enslaving others? For a congenial family life, it is imperative that there is an agreement between husband and wife, father and son, and brothers and sisters regarding the extent of freedom each should enjoy.

Here, we are not discussing absolute freedom, for no social relationship can be completely independent. It is the relative freedom which is essential, because without it the capacity of a person is blunted and the graph of his work competence also goes down. Just as an excess of freedom is a problem, so is the excess of dependence. Can we create a family dynamics with a balance of both freedom and dependence?

Interdependence

The second principle of the philosophy of non-absolutism is our relative dependence on each other. While the anatomical structure of the human body is a good example of such dependence, the mental disposition is not. Although man can't survive without such dependence, yet on account of his ego, a husband thinks that he can do without his wife or vice versa. When such a mentality finds manifestation in his or her verbal expression, the family gets infected with a virus. The law of Nature enjoins on the couple the necessity of relativity—the husband needs the wife and the wife the husband. A neglect of this law of Nature leads people to disrespect relativity in familial relations. They convert their sweet life into a bitter one and render it devoid of all harmony and congeniality.

Relative dependence is the great truth of life. But the ego of man or woman tries to belie this truth and this affects family life. Gripped by the disease of ego, man considers himself to be uppermost, and hence it becomes difficult for him to maintain conciliatory relationships with others. The institution of the family is built on the foundation of collectivistic disposition rather than the individualistic one. Although the collectivistic way of thinking is flowing through the atmosphere, individualism is still increasing on Earth. Those who are intellectually developed and have wealth and power do not like to work collectively with others. They even transgress the legitimate limit of the individualistic realm. The new civilization originating in the glaciers of intellectualism, wealth and power is eradicating the system of joint family by denying the value of relative independence. It is destroying the plant, both root and branch, of a graceful and harmonious life.

Reconciliation and Concordance

The third principle of the application of the philosophy of non-absolutism is reconciliation and concordance. Man's life is a museum of paradoxes and contradictions. One cannot expect to see complete uniformity in it. If a person thinks that all should have identical dispositions, identical attitudes, identical ethical norms and identical behaviour, what is it but a daydream? Equality and inequality, diversity and non-diversity are stark realities. One who denies them cannot attain peace and happiness. The golden principle of living a happy and congenial life, notwithstanding the contradictory and paradoxical situations, is reconciliation. A person imbued with an enlightened outlook can work in harmony even with the diverse dispositions, thoughts, conduct and behaviour of others.

Do you believe in mental equipoise or balance of mind? If the answer is yes, you can succeed in bringing about harmony among people with contradictory thinking. The main principle of the attainment of mental equipoise is the development of the consciousness of equanimity. When we compare the problems of an individual with those of a family, there is not much of a difference. The problems of an individual are also the problems of a family and vice-versa.

MODERATION

Although an emphasis on virtues is certainly the fundamental need of good family life, these virtuous ideals can scarcely be considered in isolation. A family is surely affected by the community and society in general. Can there be virtuous ideals in a family situation when virtue and vice exist together in the society? Indeed, for every family virtue, there exists a corresponding vice in society—for example, love your brother versus hate your neighbour, peace with your relative versus war with another community, and so on.

Are vices inevitable? The answer is yes. Vices are based on a behavioural foundation, namely, the instinctual dynamics of punishment. Rewards or leniency are punitively withheld in response to behaviour that is judged not suitably solicitous or submissive. There are three distinct groups of such punishments: (1) wrath-tyranny-persecution-oppression generated vices; (2) evil-cunning-ugliness-hypocrisy generated moralistic vices; and (3) anger-hatred-prejudice-belligerence generated humanistic vices.

A good family life in general represents the mean value interposed between defect and excess of an individual and the society in which he exists, an aspect favouring moderation in so far as choosing the middle ground is concerned. Indeed, a good family positions itself against all vices of excess, mirroring point-for-point the hierarchy of the virtues. Pride or Flattery is moderated with Shame or Criticism; Vanity or Adulation with Humiliation or Ridicule; Conceit or Patronization with Mortification or Scorn; Pretension or Indulgence with Anguish or Mockery; Impudence or Envy with Insolence or Disdain; Arrogance or Jealousy with Audacity or Contempt; Impetuosity or Covetousness with Rashness or Reproach; Presumption or Longing with Boldness or Chagrin; and finally, Smugness or Affectation with Harshness or Bitterness.

The root of the problem is a supine[2] desire to get more, even after getting enough. This desire for more is an endless and directionless journey of discontentment. Infinite is the potential power of our Will. A large portion of the power, however, lies dormant—some portion is supine and only a very small fraction is active. Our primal drives constantly demand appropriate action, and we continue to satisfy the need of the urges. The sedative of the sensual pleasures further weakens our willpower. The only way to awaken and develop is to stop feeding it through the exertion of self-discipline. When the Will is supine, we nourish sensual desires and delude ourselves into believing that pleasure is happiness.

When the Will is partly awakened, a desire for self-discipline and spiritual awareness is born. We begin to discriminate between what is good and what is evil. True, we would still be affected by external temptations and may sometimes succumb to them, but in due course, the Will becomes fully awakened and our attitudes, thoughts and perceptions begin to rotate around the nucleus of reasoning and rational conduct. Once we stop succumbing to our sensual desires, our supine Will begins to awaken from its stupor. The stranglehold of delusion is first weakened, and then destroyed. We become alert and vigilant towards truth and discipline. Then the vigilant rational mind becomes strong enough to regulate the responses to the insistence of instinctive drives and demands of carnal desires.

Once we have fully awakened our supine Will, we have to reinforce its power with determination and self-discipline. Thus strengthened, our rational mind will establish its supremacy. It will then be able to regulate our responses to even the most powerful urges and drives. Environmental conditions may temporarily influence our behaviour, but the power of the Will and rational mind is supreme. Self-discipline acts as a defending fort against the onslaught of contamination through carnal desires. Ultimately, external environment also fails to influence the behaviour of one who is self-disciplined.

When one gets pleasure from an object or a person for some time, a new quest to get pleasure from another object or another person begins soon after, and this goes on endlessly. This is the pathetic story of relationship between an individual and an object or another person in family life. No external object can take an individual to a region where he feels absolutely contented. This sense of discontentment is at the root of modern familial maladies such as economic competition, divorce, familial discord, and so on.

Fickleness, fantasy, suspiciousness and intense emotional upsurge play the role of villain in making family life unhappy and wretched. If there is a question as to how life in a family can be made happy, the answer is in the study of the minds of the members of the family.

IMPRINTS OF THE PAST

Here it is appropriate to understand the concept of mind. You have to differentiate between mind and consciousness. Mind itself is devoid of consciousness. It does the function of consciousness by being reflected from the psyche, which is a part of consciousness. To understand mind, we must understand psyche. The mind is ephemeral. It is neither permanent nor stable. It is created and it perishes. The word 'mind' relates to the mental abilities of a human, the will, intellect, wit, power of judgement, cogitation separating capability, experiences, education, the ability to discover coherences and the communicative aspects of the human being, like language. Basically mind and psyche work together. Psyche can be accessed by the mind and mind can uncover the distortions of reality that psyche is adapted to. The psyche is a permanent entity. It is by and large healthy. A healthy psyche knows fear but doesn't allow fear to control it.

Psyche has two main functions. It is both a non-material hard disk that stores memories and a non-material digestion organ that masters fear. Psyche can be of different complexities and, in this respect, it can be compared to a mirror globe that has more or less reflectors on its surface. A globe with less mirrors gives a simple image of reality whilst a globe with many mirrors gives a highly complex image of reality. It is obvious that a highly complex psyche is able to represent reality in a more sophisticated way, but on the other hand, it is also more prone to distorted images of reality.

A strong distortion of reality can lead to a state in which temporarily the psyche does not perform its basic functions and fear is no longer digested correctly. A pathologically working psyche will not only sustain distortions of reality but also intensify them, so that help from outside is necessary (psychoanalysis) to re-enable the psyche to sanely digest fear again. As a consequence of this help, distortion of reality (that always happens because of fear) can be abolished little by little.

Superficially, it seems paradoxical that the psyche is constructed in a way so as to primarily store distorted images of reality, but it is only under these conditions that the consciousness is needed and developed. Consciousness is capable of discovering discrepancies between memories and reality and capable of correcting the distortions of reality with the help of the mind.

After the mind and the psyche, the next important factor is sacraments (samskaras). They are the retention of the effects of past deeds. In other words, retained memories become samskaras. Samskaras are responsible for conducting the course of life. From the subconscious level, these memories rise to the forefront and affect behaviour. Samskaras also result in biased attitudes. Biased attitudes precipitated as prejudices are the greatest impediments in the congeniality and concordance of family life. A husband's prejudices become an obstacle for a wife, and vice versa. The generation gap also poses its own problems. A father's prejudices will not be acceptable to a son or daughter. Such mentality of bias eventually leads to family disorder.

Here, a distinction has to be made from the sixteen sacraments mentioned in scriptures. These range from conception to funeral ceremonies: (1) Sacrament of impregnation (garbhadhan); (2) second or third month of pregnancy (punsavanam); (3) between the fifth and eighth month of pregnancy (simantonnayana); (4) the time when the child is born (jatakarma); (5) naming the child (namakarana); (6) the time the child is brought out of the house from the place of birth and initial caring (niskramana); (7) the first feeding of cereal at six months (annaprashana); (8) first cutting of hair in the first or third year (chudakarma); (9) piercing the ears in the third or fifth year (karnavedha); (10) investiture of religious sacrament from eighth year (upanayana); (11) when studies are completed (samavartana); (12) marriage ceremony (vivaha samskara); (13) sacraments relating to householders (grihasthashrama); (14) renouncing the householder's life (vanprasthashrama); (15) leading the life of a monk (sanyasashrama); and finally, the last rites of the dead (antyeshti). These are essentially rituals marked by certain sacrifices. It is believed that by virtue of performing these, the life of the performer receives a higher sanctity. Just as gold and diamonds that are dug out from the ore need refining and polishing in order to shine in all their splendour, man too needs these samskaras or pacificator ceremonies in order to shine in his best form physically, psychically and spiritually.

There are multiple layers of our psychological being.[3] In the centre is our soul, our inner being, our true self. This is who we really are, and in an ideal world, this is what we would experience and express from the moment of our birth.

However, due to our massively conditioned childhood realities, we are rarely allowed access to this aspect of our being. Therefore, our soul reacts to externally conditioned realities, creating a thick shell around our innermost being composed of various survival strategies and control dramas. Most of our repressions, fixations, denials, traumas, and neuroses are held within this layer. We could call this the disowned self.

A third layer is our social persona. It is the smiling mask behind which lie the deeply repressed aspects of our disowned self. We often become so adept at living from our social persona that few are able to penetrate the masks of success, poise, and self-control to see the pain beneath. Often, the bigger the mask, the deeper is the pain. It is only when we risk taking off the mask and explore the roots of our pain that we move towards experiencing our true self.

As we experience our true self, the healing of our disowned self can begin, and the need for our social persona dissolves. We become transparent beings able to access and reflect the light of our souls. In Indian culture, samskaras refer to dysfunctional patterns that trace their origins not only to childhood and birth traumas, but also to generations of family traditions. The law of Karma is related to these samskaras. According to the law of Karma, every moment lived unconsciously creates samskaras, or Karmic imprints, where the light from the soul gets dimmed. Some are like lines drawn in water, which are immediately cleared. Others are like lines drawn on sand. They remain for a while until the tide comes in and washes them clean. Yet others are like lines etched in stone.

These are the ones that replicate themselves lifetime after lifetime, always attracting similar energy patterns, and creating misery. These samskaras are the dark soot in an otherwise clear lamp that obstructs the light of our inner self from shining through.

In our lives, similar situations occur repeatedly and we respond to them in the same way. But each one of us responds differently to any given situation because everyone has a different background. Regardless of how each one responds, if the response accompanies strong emotions like fear, hurt, etc., that emotion remains even after the situation is over. Later, when a similar situation revisits this emotional impression (samskara), the same emotion is revived from the memory and the same response evoked. Furthermore, this emotional charge grows stronger each time and attracts similar situations. This is because the samskara, or the emotional charge stored in the memory, is a vibrating energy that attracts the same frequency by the force of resonance. Indeed, our past is our future. The past winds itself through the present and manifests into the future. To be free from the hold of our past, we have to cleanse the samskara.

Samskara reduces us into a programme. We live just as we are programmed. Unlimited possibilities lie before us but we respond to our life only in one stereotyped way and lose sight of all the other possibilities. All our fear is either about the unknown or about losing our knowledge. That's why we lose all our knowledge and understanding when we are caught in the fear of something. When we start responding to our life with fear, we lose our own choice, and it is from this point that our whole life starts. Everything starts to feel old and boring. What is a family but a bundle of collective experiences or samskara?

By working on past emotions and cleansing them (samskara shuddhi), life becomes different, perception of the world changes, living becomes easier and many answers to the problems of our life emerge. Emotions still come, but they don't have the same influence any more. When we cleanse samskara, our heart flowers. We become connected to Oneness, and all differences disappear. We are able to relate with people and really love them.

EMANCIPATION THROUGH AHIMSA

Mahavir understood the roots of violence in the human psyche. His warning, therefore, was against absolutism and dogmatism. His stress on Anekantvada was a plea for the recognition of the multifaceted nature of reality. The perception of reality depends on the time, place, nature and state of the viewer. Absolute truth cannot result from any one viewpoint alone. For Mahavira, absolutism was an act of mental violence.

Training in non-violence is essential to make the family environment healthy. Training in behaviour infused with morality and humility is a part and parcel of this training. We are interpreting ahimsa in a very narrow sense. Though the first foundation of non-violence is 'Do not kill anyone' and 'Do not torture anyone', the multi-storied mansion of ahimsa has: (1) verbal non-violence as its first storey; (2) mental non-violence as its second storey; and (3) emotional non-violence as its third storey. In this manner, true understanding becomes possible.

It has been said that an angry person opens his mouth and closes his eyes. It is our mind that needs control. Wars, they say, begin in the minds of men. So it is there that peace must be won. While verbal non-violence can be experienced directly, non-violence at the internal level—mental and emotional—is difficult to grasp.

VERBAL VIOLENCE

The verbal violence is of many kinds, such as harsh words (such words act like a sharp weapon rending the heart), taunting or satirical words (words uttered without due deliberation), and words that hurt others. All these types of words can never unite two hearts but tear them apart.

At this point, we would like to recall the saying of poet Thiruvalluvar, who lived during the same period as Mahavir. Thiruvalluvar composed 1330 kurals. One of them tells us how spoken words can create non-violence in thought and action. It says,

யாகாவா ராயினும் நாகாக்க காவாக்கால்
சோகாப்பர் சொல்லிழுக்குப் பட்டு.

Restraining the tongue is an important virtue to be followed by every human being, since uncontrolled words can cause immense damage to others and ultimately to oneself. Biblical support for these lines can be had in Proverbs 12:13; 'Wicked are snared by the transgression of their lips.' Verbal violence acts as a wood-worm in family life. Just as the wood-worm continuously eats away the wood, similarly, verbal violence gnaws at the thread of familial affection and bonds. To prevent verbal non-violence, we recommend a five-fold policy of using: (1) polite language; (2) sweet language; (3) innocent language; (4) unbiased language; and (5) prudent language.

The basic element that unites a family is mutual trust. Habitual lying hits at the root of trust. Trust unites two into one and breach of trust splits two into two hundred. The most harmful action that divides the family is falsehood. Training in truthfulness or integrity is as essential as training in non-violence. The mind has three main functions: (1) memory or recalling; (2) imagination or planning; and (3) thinking. Memory is inevitable for one's development. Looking from the Anekanta perspective, forgetting is also as essential as recalling. Anekantvada is a vision within which the paradox of all opposites is integrated. If we look at things with balance, we will know that opposites are complementary to each other. Without opposites there is no growth and awareness. When we are aware of the cycle of opposites, we don't see them as opposites. We see them as compatible for growth, allowing us to approach the world openly. In family life, there might be incidents of exchange of hot or unpleasant words and unpleasant behaviour. If family members are not trained in the art of forgetting, these incidents can be instrumental in disintegrating the family.

A person who has the ability to obliterate the memory of unpleasant behaviour can not only remain tension-free himself or herself but can also do the same for other members of the family. Unpleasant behaviour creates restlessness in one's heart and a restless heart creates mental tension. The mental tension of one individual can become instrumental in making other members of the family unhappy and tense.

Egoism is not a direct form of violence, but it definitely plays the role of a pair of scissors, which cuts the very threads of familial virtues. The truth as to why a person becomes an egoist is very difficult to investigate. Despite being aware of the transitory nature of his fortunes, he shuts his eyes to the stark reality and behaves as if attainments, of which he is proud, are permanent things. A person's egoistic attitude generates an inferiority complex in other family members, which in turn gives rise to reactionary violence.

MAMATVA AS A VICE

The feeling of mamatva (affection or attachment) is not a direct form of violence, but is perhaps the greatest cause of violence. The human tendency to acquire excessive wealth and possessions is so mean, rigid and tight that it cannot spare even a little space to accommodate any noble mentality. It is manifested in practical life in the form of economic conflict. For example, a father due to his relatively more mamatva towards one or more of his children may show partiality in distributing wealth among his children. Such action may give rise to violence as a reaction. It also makes the environment in the family full of disgust and agony. There is an intimate relationship between behaviour and distribution of wealth, etc., in the family. If the distribution of resources happens to be unbiased and equal, the father's behaviour will be considered just and congenial. If not, it will shake the foundation of concordance in the family.

INTOLERANCE

In the context of modern familial relations, should we not accept the reality that the virtue of tolerance has been lost? Tolerance is seen as a weakness. It certainly reflects the egoistic psyche of this age. However, let us be clear that economic and intellectual development without tolerance are not going to yield auspicious fruits.

There is an old story but the truth embodied in it is not outdated. Once, a king asked his prime minister to find out why the business community in his kingdom was healthier and happier than him. After thorough research, the prime minister submitted his findings. The king was astonished to know that the businessmen of his kingdom were very tolerant. Reflecting on this, the king's behaviour underwent a change. His health improved and his joy reflected on his face.

There might be multiple factors responsible for the disunity of families today, but the root cause is intolerance. Two individuals can live together and still be unable to tolerate each other. Is it not cowardice camouflaged? Whether it is business failure, examinations, or family discords, people tend to go to the extreme, endangering even lives. In the context of social development, this condition is reflective of shared degradation of community living.

The family is an institution. What do we gain if it exists and what do we lose if it fumbles? Both aspects are worth examining. Can a person live alone? If he could, why would he accept the bondage of relationships? Can a lonely person not feel content? If he could, why would he take upon himself the burden of others' discontent? The reality is that no human being can live alone.

The first law of Nature is that man and woman are two living beings. The second law of Nature is that the union of man and woman perpetuates mankind. There cannot be any rule in the life of a person who leads an altogether solitary life. As soon as two persons live together, a number of rules come into existence, and the number goes on increasing.

Some of them are natural, others are man-made. The problem is that a systematic training of both is missing. No one can live together peacefully unless they are tolerant of others.

The parents are the nucleus of a family. If their behaviour is refined, it gets reflected in their children. Children can never be like their parents. Though they inherit their genes, they are still different. Being too concerned or preoccupied about economic matters, parents fail to train their children. More and more people are growing up as 'individuals'; the collective consciousness is drying up. Many young people today are so engrossed in their own imagination that they are not grateful to their parents and plainly ignore other elderly family members. There is hardly any sense of obligation seen in them towards elderly people. Youths in prosperous families do provide their elders the requisite means of living, but polite and affectionate behaviour is often missing. How can the emotionally parched atmosphere of 'Homes for the Old' substitute for families? It is so strange that while people are showing increasing sensitivity towards animals and strangers afflicted with disease and disability, they are less sensitive to members of their own family. Even tolerance has the same pattern. People tolerate rudeness and outright insults from strangers but pounce on their own family members for the mildest indiscretions.

Spouses should have only that much expectation from each other which does not obstruct their individual health, interest and thinking. The perennial problem that stems out of infatuation with something or someone is that one weaves a huge web of hopes and desires, but when harsher times come and these hopes and desires are not fulfilled, intolerance becomes very intense. Hence, we feel that a tolerant individual leads to a tolerant family. A tolerant family leads to a tolerant society, and a tolerant society gives birth to a tolerant nation. And tolerant nations form a tolerant world.

Right faith (samyag darshana)[4] is a value of utmost importance for the establishment of peaceful coexistence. It can be developed by imparting training in Anekanta. We must give up insistence on one-sided views. The tendency to persist in one's viewpoint, thinking and decision breeds a feeling of discord in the heart of the other person.

Flexibility of nature is an important virtue of a man's personality. There is an element of pleasantness in this world but its application is not so pleasant. It appears that man has bolted the doors of his ego; he has no windows through which the fresh air of other people's views can enter. The fact that the frenzy of anger destroys a family is only secondary. The primary truth is the ego that generates the frenzy of anger.

CONTEMPLATION AND RECONCILIATION

The mysteries of faith are degraded if they are made into an object of affirmation and negation, when in reality they should be an object of contemplation. There is always a cycle of rise and fall. The peak of prosperity ultimately leads to decline. The culmination of poverty leads to prosperity.

When the excess reaches its climax, the road ahead is likely to reach a dead end. We may choose to ignore the rules of Nature, but we cannot escape them. The storm of consumerism is blowing across the planet at a terrific speed. Words like self-restraint, renunciation, integrity, and fixing a limit to our needs and desires are losing importance. When such words lose their meaning, the fall ahead becomes not only inevitable but also imminent. Externally, everything appears to be doing exceedingly well, but deep inside a process of antithesis has already begun.

The surge of consumerism and hedonism is the root cause of the gradual waning of the power of tolerance. The secondary consequence of intolerance is deterioration of mental strength and perseverance. In civilization's progress, mental strength and perseverance play a dominant role. No culture can cope with a difficult situation or advance without them. People with a lavish lifestyle, too much affluence, abundant means of ease and comfort and immense luxury invariably become mentally weak and timid, even when faced with ordinary sickness. It becomes impossible for them to abandon their comforts, and comfort and moral courage are generally mutually exclusive.

Both desire (kama) and money (artha) play a vital role in the rise and fall of society. As far as the management of wealth is concerned (arthvyavastha), there have been many thinkers who have pondered over the modification and amelioration of economic systems. For example, thinkers like Adam Smith (1723–1790) and Karl Marx (1818–1883) gave great insights into economic systems. But little has been done to understand the management of human passions and desires.

A person who has not refined or sublimated his kama will live a perturbed life of restlessness, discontentment and mental agitation. On the other hand, one who has succeeded in refining and sublimating his kama will live a life of peace, contentment, ecstasy and composure. Absolute freedom from kama does not appear plausible for a human being living in the world of sensory feasts but sublimation and refinement of kama is certainly possible.

Once, a saint gifted with supernatural powers (siddha) arrived in a village. Learning about his power to fulfil any wish, a multitude of people gathered around him to have their wishes fulfilled. A woman in her fifties came and wished to be a young lady so that she could be attractive to her husband. The siddha said, 'Be it so,' and she turned into a nymph. When her husband, a poor peasant, saw her he became very angry and admonished her for opting to be a nymph rather than asking for wealth and comfort. He went to the siddha and wished for his wife to become a female donkey. The siddha said, 'Be it so', and the peasant's wife at once became a female ass and started grazing in the field. After a while, when the son of the peasant arrived and saw a female ass grazing in the field, he scolded his father for not being vigilant. When his father narrated the entire story, the astonished son went to the siddha and asked for his mother to be reinstated in her original form. The siddha said, 'Be it so,' and the ass got transformed into the old woman again. What is the moral of the story? There is no place for selfishness and anger in a family.

PURIFICATION OF EMOTIONS

There are two main causes of familial conflict—wealth and behaviour. Man's attitude and behaviour are immensely affected by the expansion of the world of material objects. Money is the main means of obtaining these objects. Hence, economic achievements take centre stage in life and attitudes and behaviour get moulded accordingly.

The most important factor responsible for peace in a family is humble, modest, unassuming and sweet behaviour. One of the layers of the human mind is the reptilian brain.[5] To become human, the reptilian brain must be brought under control. What is essential for human behaviour is the purification of his stream of emotions.

Anger, egotism, greed and fear are negative tendencies that play a dominant role in making one's behaviour distorted and negative. These tendencies can be purified only at a deeper level of our consciousness. If the consciousness can be awakened at a deeper level, anger can be changed into forgiveness and tolerance; egoistic attitude can be changed into humility and sweetness; greed can be changed into contentment; and fear can be changed into friendship. Those who think of creating a beautiful home must start from a beautiful mind first. It is only then that they can make a family an ideal one.

No family can live happily on the basis of mere economic prosperity. The seeds of happiness are hidden in the right form of emotional development. Transformation of inner consciousness is essential. Just as a family needs money for its sustenance, meditation is essential for inner transformation. A good family is poised over a tripod of financial sustenance, happiness and mental peace of its members. Mutual cooperation in fulfilling familial needs and availability of resources, a strong base and assurance for the family, and mutual trust and feeling of satisfaction amongst members are the three hallmarks of an integrated family. Contemplation and reconciliation are two powerful techniques to achieve and preserve integration.

THE SECRET OF PEACE

Once there were two kings. The kingdom of one king was notorious for discords, conflicts and quarrels. Distressed by this awful situation, he went to the neighbouring king and expressed his anguish before him. He asked the other king whether there were any discords, conflicts and quarrels in his kingdom. The other king replied, 'No, Sir, not at all.' 'How is it so? In my kingdom, I am fed-up with the strife and conflicts that occur every day. How do you manage to remain immune from such a situation?' asked the frustrated king.

'My kingdom is guarded by four security guards. The first guard is Truth. No citizen of my country indulges in any form of unrighteous act. No one indulges in unethical practices like false weights and measures. My second guard is Justice. No one does another any injustice. The elderly members of my kingdom are not unjust towards the younger ones nor are the younger ones unjust towards the elderly members of my kingdom. Affection is my third security guard. The mutual relations between all people are marked by love and sweetness. Thus O King, there is neither unrighteous behaviour nor exploitation. The fourth guard is Sacrifice. My people observe altruism. Selfishness dare not face it.' Thus the bewildered king came to know the secret of peace amongst people.

HOW TO CONTAIN SELFISHNESS

Once there was a curious youth who heard of a village where all families lived in peace. When he entered the village, he felt a kind of peace and serenity he had seldom experienced earlier. He asked a young man the reason for this peace. The young man replied, 'Friend, my people are truly religious.' 'But I see religious people quarrelling a lot,' this man protested. 'Such people are not truly religious, they are only followers of certain conventions, beliefs and rituals,' the villager replied. 'In what way are the people truly religious here?' asked the visitor. 'Every villager here posesses a worshiping place with four gates. We enter only through these gates and practise our Dharma,' the villager replied. 'Which are the four gates?' the visitor asked, to which the young man replied, 'The first gate is called Forgiveness. Only he can enter the worshiping place who has cultivated the power of forbearance and shuns all forms of disagreeable treatment or insulting behaviour towards others. The second gate is Freedom from reactive behaviour. It enjoins on the people to consume and utilize materialistic objects without getting attached to them. The third gate is Ingenuousness. Our mutual dealings are infused with the spirit of ingenuousness. Our behaviour is frank. No one deceives the other. Since our behaviour is free from hypocrisy or affectation, we are people of integrity. No one indulges in false weights and measures. The fourth gate is Modesty. All of us behave amicably and gently with others. The thread of gentleness and modesty keeps us united.'

Finally the visitor asked, 'Who is the deity worshipped here?' 'The name of the deity is Righteousness (dharma devata).' 'How is the idol created?' 'The idol of Righteousness is made from the alloy of three metals: ahimsa, self-restraint and austerity. By worshipping it, we have been blessed with the knowledge of amity and the power of self-restraint. All the villagers exercise restraint over consumption even though we have a lot to consume. There is neither a superiority complex nor any inferiority complex. The worship of Dharma blessed us with the boon of austerity. We are not comfort-loving. We know how to live a hard life. We do not play truant from toil. We make little use of the means of comfort, so most of our people are very healthy. We constantly endeavour for emotional development. This makes us mentally healthy too. Our village is inhabited by good families. This is the reason that you find an environment of peace here.' The visitor said, 'Friend, you have given me a new philosophy, a new outlook. It is now that I have got an opportunity to be acquainted with the real form of Dharma. I will also try that my village follows your example and we all breathe in the air of happiness emanating from coexistence.'

NEW DIRECTION: EMOTIONAL INTELLIGENCE

People understand in a very direct and instinctive way that intelligence is fundamental and plays a key role in effectiveness in life and in the ability to formulate deeper questions, the pursuit of which leads man in the direction of meaning. Thus, the idea that some people or groups of people are inherently and unalterably better endowed than others—and the deep fears and tribal rivalries and hatreds that this leads to—is completely unacceptable in supposedly civilized people.

Emotional intelligence describes an ability, capacity, or skill to perceive, assess, and manage the emotions of one's self, of others, and of groups. Capacity to perceive and understand emotions is indeed a new intelligence that includes the capacity to accurately perceive and use emotions to facilitate thinking, understand emotional meanings, and manage emotions.

The initial, most basic area has to do with the nonverbal reception and expression of emotion. Evolutionary biologists and psychologists have pointed out that emotional expression evolved in animal species as a form of crucial social communication. Facial expressions such as happiness, sadness, anger, and fear were universally recognizable in human beings. Emotion researchers, evolutionary biologists, specialists in nonverbal behaviour and others have made tremendous inroads into understanding how human beings recognize and express emotions. The capacity to accurately perceive emotions in the face or voice of others provides a crucial starting point for more advanced understanding of emotions.

The second area appears every bit as basic as the first. This is the capacity of the emotions to enter into and guide the cognitive system and promote thinking. For example, cognitive scientists pointed out that emotions prioritize thinking. In other words, something we respond to emotionally is something that grabs our attention. Having a good system of emotional input, therefore, should help direct thinking towards matters that are truly important. As a second example, a number of researchers have suggested that emotions are important for certain kinds of creativity to emerge. For example, both mood swings and positive moods have been implicated in the capacity to carry out creative thought.

Emotions convey information. Happiness usually indicates a desire to join with other people; anger indicates a desire to attack or harm others; fear indicates a desire to escape, and so forth. Each emotion conveys its own pattern of possible messages and actions associated with those messages. A message of anger, for example, may mean that the individual feels he has been treated unfairly. The anger, in turn, might be associated with specific sets of possible actions: peacemaking, attacking, retribution and revenge-seeking, or withdrawal to seek calmness. Understanding emotional messages and the actions associated with them is one important aspect of this skill.

Once a person can identify such messages and potential actions, the capacity to reason with these emotional messages and actions becomes important as well. Fully understanding emotions, in other words, involves the comprehension of the meaning of emotions, coupled with the capacity to reason with these meanings. This aspect is central to emotionally intelligent skills.

Finally, emotions can often be managed. A person needs to understand emotions to convey information. To the extent that it is under voluntary control, a person may want to remain open to emotional signals so long as they are not too painful, and block out those that are overwhelming. In between, within the person's emotional comfort zone, it becomes possible to regulate and manage one's own and others' emotions so as to promote personal and social goals.

FOUR KEY AREAS

The first and most important need for a happy family is love. Ideally, it is an unselfish love that brings a man and woman together to form a home, and ideally it is love that increases that happiness with children. The love that binds a family together is partly an impulse of nature, but in a happy home, the love is far more unselfish than a mere natural impulse. A man must not hesitate to sacrifice his own pleasures, even his life, to assure the happiness and welfare of his wife. The same unselfish love should be reciprocated by the wife. And as parents, both husband and wife should have the same unselfish love for their children.

Unfortunately, however, love can wither and die. To keep it alive and warm requires close association, attention and care. When both parents work and have little time for their children, they become, in a measure, strangers to them. By nature, children love their parents and long for their parents' love in return. Warm personal love which expresses itself in affectionate association, care, and attention prevents such estrangements and bitterness, and is the single greatest source of happiness in the home. No amount of money, fast cars, gifts, and gadgets can substitute for it.

The second key word to happiness is faith. Faith, in all its aspects of trust, confidence and reliance, brings happiness. If a home is to be happy, parents must conduct themselves in such a way that they can have implicit faith in each other and also inspire such faith in their children. If parents by personal example show their commitment to a virtuous life, they instinctively win the confidence of their children, and children likewise hold the confidence of their parents. They believe in one another.

The third key word to happiness is self-discipline. Self-discipline is acquired only gradually and sometimes painfully through external discipline. A generation ago, we entered the age of permissiveness, when children were allowed to make their own decisions and do their own thing. Today, psychiatrists almost universally agree that instead of making children happier, this permissiveness has had tragic results for both children and parents. Until children reach enough maturity in judgment and character to administer self-discipline, they must be guided by their parents. Obedience implies definite restrictions. Parents must emphasize to their children that some things are right and some things are wrong, and see to it that they observe the limitations. But when instruction fails and discipline seems necessary, it must never be done through frustration or anger but always with love.

The fourth key word to happiness is responsibility. Responsibility grows naturally out of the first three. If a home is filled with love, with mutual confidence and trust, and has had the guidance and correction necessary to develop self-discipline, the natural result is recognition of responsibility. Each member of the family feels a responsibility towards the others, a responsibility to merit confidence and truth, to keep one's promises, and to carry out duties and assignments. As this sense of responsibility becomes a habit, it carries over to those outside the family, to employers, associates, and friends. When members of a family have little or no confidence in one another, when they seldom depend on doing what they are supposed to do, you have the making of unhappiness and tragedy. But when members of a family have full confidence in each other, and when through self-discipline they have formed the habit of responsibility, you have the sure foundation, not only of a happy family, but of successful lives.

As we are discussing natural ways to generate happiness in a home, we would like to share a famous story interlinking wealth, success and love.

The Choice

A woman came out of her house and saw three old men with long white beards sitting in her front yard. She did not recognize them. She said, 'I don't think I know you, but you must be hungry. Please come in and have something to eat.'

'Is the man of the house home?' they asked.

'No', she replied. 'He's out.'

'Then we cannot come in,' they replied.

In the evening when her husband came home, she told him what had happened. 'Go tell them I am home and invite them in!' the husband said.

The woman went out and invited the men in. 'We do not go into a house together,' they replied. 'Why is that?' she asked. One of them explained: 'His name is Wealth,' he said, pointing to one of his friends, and pointing to the other, he said, 'He is Success, and I am Love.' Then he added, 'Now go in and discuss with your husband which one of us you want in your home.' The woman went in and told her husband what the old man had said. Her husband was overjoyed. 'How nice!', he said. 'If that is the case, let us invite Wealth. Let him come and fill our home with wealth!' His wife disagreed. 'My dear, why don't we invite Success?' Their daughter was listening from the other corner of the house. She jumped in with her own suggestion: 'Would it not be better to invite Love? Our home will then be filled with love!' 'Let us heed our daughter's advice,' said the husband to his wife. 'Go out and invite Love to be our guest.' The woman went out and asked the three old men, 'Which one of you is Love? Please come in and be our guest.' Love got up and started walking towards the house. The other two also got up and followed him. Surprised, the lady asked Wealth and Success, 'I only invited Love, why are you coming in?' The old men replied together, 'If you had invited Wealth or Success, the remaining two of us would have stayed out, but since you invited Love, wherever He goes, we go with him. Wherever there is Love, there is also Wealth and Success!'

HOW TO BRING ABOUT CHANGE

There are three stages in the process of awakening.[6] The first stage is the formation of an idea or thought (vichara). We have to create a system of healthy and strong ideas. The second stage is transforming the thoughts or ideas into imprints on the subconscious level of mind (samskara). The third stage is conduct (aachara) to put principles into practice. The gulf between percept (vichara) and practice (aachara) is only natural. Only those who are free from passion can practise what they preach. There is always a discrepancy between the speech and practice of a person who remains engrossed in attachment (raga) and aversion (dvesha), and this gulf between his thought and deed cannot be removed. It is only through a bridge that people can cross a river. We have to have a bridge in the form of samskara to remove the gap between thought and action. We recommend a process of change. We recommend the application of the Anekanta view in practical life. It will prove as a protective armour for peace in a family. The combination of prudently consuming resources and freedom from attachment to things constitutes the best alternative. There have been many attempts to build a new social order but the focus has always been to change the external structure of society. Any attempt to change only the system of society without changing mental attitudes will not succeed.

There are four constituents of the path to liberation: (1) Right knowledge; (2) Right faith; (3) Right conduct; and (4) Right penance. A spiritual practitioner can attain liberation by an integrated practice of the above four. He can steadily march forward according to his own competence by sincere self-effort. However, no one is bound by it. The possibility of gradation and amalgamation of self-restraint and penance is so vast that the dedicated practice of the above can be undertaken in the simplest form possible. Faith is concerned with mental attitude, which is free from the distinction between the simple and the difficult. Right knowledge consists in the basic understanding of the ultimate truth that every human being is always separate and yet deeply connected with others.

ALWAYS SEPARATE, ALWAYS CONNECTED

There is a fundamental separateness and connectedness of all human beings in a way that is both universally applicable and culturally sensitive. William James (1842–1910) said, 'The community stagnates without the impulse of the individual. The impulse dies away without the sympathy of the community.' For Mahatma Gandhi (1869 1948), interdependence was as much the ideal of man as was self-sufficiency. 'Man is a social being. Without interrelation with society he cannot realize his oneness with the Universe or suppress his egotism. His social interdependence enables him to test his faith and to prove himself on the touchstone of reality.' Stephen Covey[7] traced a personal development outline from dependence in childhood (many people never grow out of a dependency culture) through independence in adolescence, to an interdependence in adulthood—an outline that recognizes that if one gives one's best and works towards a common goal, with a shared mission and vision but with the freedom to use one's best judgement on how to go about achieving it, optimum results can be realized.

Independent thinking alone is not suited to interdependent reality. Independent people who do not have the maturity to think and act interdependently may be good individual producers, but they won't be good leaders or team players. A beautiful home nurtures a dependent child to grow as an independent adult. The next step forward for this independent adult is to form interdependent groups of organized effort.

So far in the book, we have tried to develop an understanding of culture and an understanding of the individual and family in terms of unity of mind and harmony of living. In the next and concluding chapter, we examine how issues of human separateness or independence and those of human connectedness or interdependence are played out in diverse cultural contexts of our country.

6

Birth of a Noble Nation

Lord, make me an instrument of Your peace; Where there is hatred let me sow love; And where there is injury, pardon; And where there is doubt, faith.

—St. Francis of Assisi

Whether it is an individual or a nation, the constant endeavour is to face the realities of the present and to prepare for the challenges of the future by drawing on the experience of the past. Look at any dialogue anywhere, in whatever discipline—you will notice in it a concern for attaining peace, progress and prosperity. Students are concerned about opportunities, farmers are worried about making both ends meet, women are worried about discrimination, common citizens are worried about rising prices and inflation. While individuals and families are concerned about such problems, nations are facing many issues threatening human species as a whole, such as energy, water shortages, environment degradation, healthcare challenges, corruption and terrorism. Peace is eluding individuals and nations and this is not only impeding their progress, but also causing restlessness of minds, giving rise to further concerns, inequalities, fear, hatred, extremism and terrorism. Unfortunately, in addition, we have not been able to cope with the problems of dissatisfaction created by some past events. We have all heard many stories of how hatred among individuals has caused irreparable harm to all those involved and their families. Nations have countless memorials, reminding us day in and day out of the havoc created by wars and the residual sentiments of wars that people have to live with for a long time. But are we learning enough? It is true that all of us realize that today's world is a connected one. Technology and travel have nearly made the world a global village. The world has to become a federation of nations. A nation is a federation of states, social groups, families and individuals. So what is needed is a situation of live and let live. One's needs, privacy, liberty, aspirations, accomplishments are all important. But there has to be a concept of a noble nation, where the welfare of the whole nation as a whole is ingrained in the thinking and actions of its people. This is the need of the hour. How do we achieve this idea of a noble nation?

Our visualization of a noble nation is two-fold. One is internal, concerned with the individual and encompassing the family, community and society. Another concerns enterprise and covers the issues of livelihood, business, distribution of wealth and respect for individual property and rights. We do not offer any new theory or postulate any new concept but draw from the heritage of our civilization. The bottom line is that a citizen with a value system respects the family, respects society, and thereby respects the nation. Furthermore, the person is conscious that he or she is a part of the world family. The operational line is the prosperity of people with adequate earning capacity. We call such a nation a developed nation. Economic prosperity and an embedded value system would promote a peaceful and prosperous society and thereby the evolution of a happy nation.

Life originated on planet Earth 600 million years ago. The continental drift occurred 200 million years ago, creating five continents. Mammals evolved 140 million years ago. The earliest human type, called Hominid, evolved 26 million years ago. Modern man evolved out of Hominid some 200,000 years ago. He migrated across the planet as hunter-gatherer before settling down in communities only in the last 50,000 years. The spoken language is some 10,000 years old while writing evolved only in the last few thousand years. Civilization, as we see it today, has emerged within the short span of 200 to 400 generations, that is, 5,000 to 10,000 years ago. Is there a genetic continuity?

Newer genetic technologies have given us better insight into retracing the history of man. In the words of Michael Hammer, Professor of Genomic Analysis at the University of Arizona, 'The DNA of a human being is his history book.' Millions of people around the world can trace their ancestry back several generations or more through oral history, family documents or government records of such events as marriages and births. The history contained in human genes also links every person on Earth to a common genetic origin in Africa. Natural variations in the genes occurred over time as people migrated out of Africa. The DNA (deoxyribonucleic acid) evolved, mutated and changed. It is probably during the 30,000-50,000 years of co-existence that societies evolved, adopting newer innovations and cultures. By the nature of human migration and mixing in the past, we have not remained separate and isolated on different continents all these years. We do have a history of migration and our genome reflects that.

So there is genetic continuity. While a gene resides in a particular chromosome, it does not necessarily remain there in the next generation. The physical material of heredity is not, as had been generally supposed, protein, but DNA. The

DNA molecule is a double helix. Its two strands have sugar-phosphate-sugar-phosphate- backbones from which paired bases extend inward towards the axis of the helix and are held together by hydrogen bonds that regularly match the bases—adenine with thymine and guanine with cytosine. The basic nature of genetic continuity is the nature of the mechanism whereby the DNA molecule replicates itself. All life comes from life of its own kind but in a unique form.

CHALLENGES OF MODERN SOCIETY

In a global population of 6 billion, only half have access to proper supply of drinking water. One third of the world's population has no access to sanitation. By 2025, the world population is going to rise to 8 billion but only one billion will have sufficient water. Five billion will have no access to sanitation. The use of fossil fuels has caused enormous problems for the environment, resulting in abnormal changes in climatic conditions. In the healthcare sector, major diseases like HIV/AIDS, cancer, tuberculosis, malaria, other water-borne diseases and coronary artery diseases have increased considerably. The rate of development has challenged the delicate balance of natural resources and set in competition at every level of human interaction. The happiness, prosperity and comforts of healthy living have become stress-laden rather than a natural way of existence.

Is creating a near disease-free, economically prosperous and peaceful society a possible proposition? In our opinion, this could be achieved through a triangular approach: (1) creation of a clean and green environment, (2) promotion of a three-dimensional lifestyle approach to healthcare coupled with genetically engineered drugs; and (3) evolution of enlightened citizens.

Creation of a Clean and Green Environment

Earth is experiencing both stratospheric cooling (due to ozone hole) and tropospheric warming (due to increased greenhouse gases). The energy production through fossil fuels leads to the generation of 30 billion tonnes of carbon dioxide annually. We have the responsibility of protecting the Earth's environment, and creating affordable alternate sources of clean energy on a scale large enough to be a perennial substitute for fossil fuels.

Stephen Hawking visualized the need to spread the human race out into space if it is to survive. We agree with him. Fixing what we are doing to the environment is no guarantee that the Earth can support our massive numbers in the long run without interruption. The best hope for our survival is to inhabitat multiple planets. The best hope that we don't go through wild economic swings from sharp changes in the relationship between energy supply and demand is to test the new ideas that can diversify our supplies in an environmentally friendly way. We think that a significant investment to test the technical and economic feasibility of space-based solar power is wise.

The return to the moon should be seen as an economic investment in our long-term future. The technology spin-offs will probably not be as great, but the new industries that will emerge in the long-term and that will help support the coming generations will be significant. Space-based solar power may eventually be cheaper for building power satellites with materials from the moon. The moon may eventually supply us with clean power from its helium-3 reserves.

Besides the moon, Mars is another celestial body that has captured the human imagination. Mars is believed to represent self-esteem, respect, energy and ego. In Indian culture, people born with certain orbital positions of Mars are believed to have a volatile temper and have difficulty in adjusting with their spouses. For nearly fifty years, our civilization has been attempting to send a spacecraft to Mars. By the beginning of the twenty-first century, only ten missions out of thirty-three had been a complete success. Mars is the fourth planet from the Sun, the next after Earth. Mars revolves around the Sun once every 687 Earth days with the length of a day very similar to that of the Earth—24 hours, 39 minutes, 35 seconds. The atmosphere is mostly carbon dioxide (95.3 percent). There is no oxygen. Mars was once Earth-like. The fingerprint of a water planet lies in its landforms. Large channels and small gullies attest to a history of flowing water. There is the possibility that life may have existed there and might even exist there today.

As we progress technologically in space missions, we have to take short-term measures for liberating ourselves from fossil fuel and leading India towards sustainable clean, green energy and environment.

Structure of Energy Sources

Based on the progress visualized for India during the next two decades, power generating capacity has to increase to 400,000 MW by 2030 from the existing 130,000 MW. Energy independence has to be achieved through three different sources, namely, hydel capacity, nuclear power and non-conventional ones (primarily solar energy)—apart from thermal power. The hydel power generated through normal water sources and interlinking of rivers is expected to contribute an additional 50,000 MW. A number of large-scale solar energy farms with a capacity of hundreds of megawatts could contribute around 55,000 MW. Nuclear power plants can have a target of 50,000 MW of power. The projected energy availability from wind energy is 64,000 MW. The balance 51,000 MW has to be generated from conventional thermal plants through clean coal technologies, gas and other renewable sources of energy such as biomass, municipal waste and solar thermal power. The most significant aspect, however, would be that power generated through renewable energy technologies has to be increased to 28 per cent against the present 5 per cent. In the transportation sector, India plans to use emulsified diesel, bio-diesel and ethanol in a big way.

This will lead to a clean and hygienic environment for we will be partially eliminating fossil material usage that generates the maximum carbon dioxide. The results that are now coming in tell us that we can live without fossil-material based fuel by using solar, nuclear, and hydro power generation. Billions of tonnes of carbon let into the Earth's atmosphere can be nearly eliminated. Similarly, by networking rivers within the states and between states and coastal areas, adequate quantity of potable, sanitation and irrigation water can be effectively provided. Increased afforestation may also lead to conditions favourable for monsoon rains. A clean and green environment will make our planet a friendlier place for humanity to thrive.

Promotion of Three-pronged Lifestyle Approach for Healthcare

In our hospitals, doctors tend to focus their attention on the treatment of body ailments to reverse pathology to physiology. It has been realized that the success rate of such treatment is only partial. A group of Indian scientists had the opportunity to experiment with the concept of mind-body approach for therapy of breast cancer patients. Their experiment revealed that the psycho-neuro immunological axis significantly influenced the prognosis of these patients. Another experimental evidence of this concept emerged from a study carried out at the Defence Research and Development Organization (DRDO) in collaboration with Global Hospital

Research Centre at Mount Abu in Rajasthan, on the regression of Coronary Artery Disease (CAD) through a three-pronged lifestyle intervention. It included (1) low-fat, high-fibre diet; (2) regular aerobic exercise; and (3) meditation. The study clearly demonstrated that lifestyle intervention resulted in regression of CAD as evidenced by the disappearance of plaque in angiograms. Every individual has an inherent spiritual potential, which lies dormant. If we invoke this potential, we can definitely enhance the process of healing and improve the quality of life of patients.

Such a three-pronged approach to healthcare will be a significant evolution in the history of healthcare philosophy and will be applicable for the treatment of diseases like HIV/AIDS, cancer, diabetes and many other chronic diseases. This lifestyle approach is not only less costly but also provides a sustainable solution for improving the quality of life of individuals.

Enlightened Citizenship and Economic Prosperity

In the book *Dialogues of Plato,* Plato states, 'our aim in founding the State was not the disproportionate happiness of any one class, but the greatest happiness of the whole.' Around the same time, 2400 years ago, Tamil poet Thiruvalluvar[1] said,

பீணீயீன்மை செல்வம் வீளைவீன்பம் ஏமம்
அணீயென்ப நாட்டிற்கீவ வைந்து

That is, 'The important elements that constitute a nation are: being disease-free; wealth; high productivity; harmonious living and strong defence.' We have to find how we can provide all these elements to the citizens of a nation on an equitable basis for the happiness of all. This may result in an extremism-free, peaceful world. We would like to first discuss how to evolve an enlightened society.

EVOLUTION OF ENLIGHTENED SOCIETY

How do we create an enlightened society, which will have three components: (1) Education with value system; (2) Religion transforming into spirituality; and (3) Economic development for societal transformation?

Education with Value System

The seeds of peace in the world have their origin in the righteousness in the heart of every individual. Such righteous citizens lead to the evolution of an enlightened society. Education has to be so designed that the righteousness in the heart is developed in young minds. The prime learning period is five to seventeen years of age. As an ancient Greek teacher said, 'Give me a child for seven years; afterwards, let God or devil take the child. They cannot change the child.' This indicates the power of great teachers and what they can inculcate in the young minds. Parents and teachers must inculcate moral values amongst children. It requires the ability to have insights into the uniqueness and universality of human consciousness. True education is the acquisition of enlightened feelings and enlightened power to understand daily events and the permanent truth linking man to his environment, human and planetary.

In 1950, Rev. Kalathil, Rector of St. Joseph's College, Tiruchirappalli, would take a class for an hour every Monday. He would talk about good human beings in the present and past and the qualities of a good human being. He would discuss Buddha, Confucius, St. Augustine, Caliph Omar, Mahatma Gandhi, Einstein, Abraham Lincoln and moral stories linked to our civilizational heritage. Father Kalathil would tell young students how these great personalities had evolved as good human beings through parental care, teaching and companionship of great books. It is essential that in schools and colleges, lectures are given by great teachers of the institution once a week for one hour on civilizational heritage and derived value system. Text books like *Jeevan Vigyan* by Acharya Mahapragya could give model lessons on values.[2] This moral science class will elevate young minds to love the country, love other human beings and elevate them to higher planes. The results of the analysis of the book *Five Minds for the Future* by Howard Gardner,[3] in our opinion, reveals the five capacities to be built in the learning process of the young:

1. *Disciplinary mind*: Disciplinary minds require mastery of major schools of thought, which may include science, mathematics, history and religion. Apart from this, the disciplinary mind has to be enriched with expertise in at least one professional field. Research confirms that it takes up to ten years to master a discipline. This mind also knows how to work steadily over time to improve skill and understanding.
2. *Synthesizing mind:* This refers to the ability to integrate ideas from different disciplines or spheres into an integrated system and communicate the synthesized thoughts. With the increasing volume of information in the present-day world, capacity to synthesize assumes great importance.
3. *Creative mind:* It is essential to build the capacity to uncover and create solutions for new problems, questions and phenomena. For examples on creativity, we look for leaders rather than managers. The creative mind puts forth new ideas, poses familiar questions and arrives at unprecedented answers. It seeks to remain at least one step ahead of even the most sophisticated computers and

robots. Most of the computers of the future and their accessories will be micro-sized, wearable and will have wireless communication with each other. Moderately priced PCs capable of performing about a billion calculations per second today will be able to perform about a trillion calculations per second within the next ten years. It is predicted that by 2019, the computational ability of an ordinary PC would exceed the capability of the human brain. By 2029, the capability of a normal PC would be around 1000 times that of the brain. Our view is that the creative mind of the human being will always be superior to the most powerful computers on the horizon.

4. *Respectful mind:* It is a uniquely developed, mature mind that has an awareness and appreciation for differences among human beings. The capacity of the respectful mind leads to an understanding of other people and mutual trust. In today's world, where we are all interlinked and need to maintain working relationships, intolerance is no longer a viable option.
5. *Ethical mind*: It is indeed a built-in capacity for fulfilling one's responsibility as a worker and as a citizen simultaneously. It will essentially lead to 'work with integrity and succeed with integrity'. The mind conceptualizes how workers can serve a purpose beyond self-interest and how citizens can work unselfishly to improve the lot of all. The ethical mind then acts on the basis of these analyses. In the present scenario, the need for the respectful mind and the ethical mind is very important because many of the societal problems today arise out of a lack of consideration for others and the overwhelming selfishness of the individual. The education system has to cultivate these minds among the youth, so that they learn to respect others, and are tolerant and persevering for realizing their goals in life.

With these five types of minds, a person will be well equipped to deal with what is expected as well as what cannot be anticipated. Without these minds, a person will be at the mercy of forces that he or she can't understand. Our educational, political, managerial and spiritual systems should nurture these five kinds of minds for cultivating positive human potential. Disciplines, syntheses and creativity can be put to all kinds of ends if we do not cultivate a sense of respect and an ethical orientation. Hence, the five kinds of minds should be made to work synergistically.

Nurturing all the five minds is possible by building five capacities among the youth. These five capacities are inquiry, creativity, application of technology and entrepreneurial and moral leadership. By developing these, we will produce the Autonomous Learner, who is a self-directed, self-controlled, lifelong learner having the capacity to respect authority and, at the same time, question it in an appropriate manner.

These Autonomous Learners would work together as a self-organizing network and transform their society into a prosperous nation. The most important part of education is to instil among the students a can-do spirit.

Religion Transforming into Spirituality

Religion has two components, theology and spirituality. Even though theology is unique to every religion, the spiritual component spreads the value to be inculcated by human beings for promoting a good life and the welfare of the society, even while pursuing a material life.

In the early 1960s, the founder of the Indian Space Research Programme, Prof. Vikram Sarabhai, and his team had located a technically ideal place, Thumba in Kerala, for space research. It was nearest to the magnetic equator, and therefore suited for ionospheric and electrojet research in upper atmosphere. However, thousands of fishing folks lived there. The place also had an ancient St. Mary Magdalene Church, the Bishop's House and a school. The political class saw it as a difficult situation. Vikram Sarabhai approached the Bishop on a Saturday evening. Rev. Father exclaimed, 'Vikram, you are asking for my children's abode, my abode and God's abode. How is it possible?' Both had a unique quality—they could smile even in difficult situations. Rev Father asked Sarabhai to come to church on Sunday morning.

In the Sunday mass, after the prayers were over, the Bishop invited Vikram Sarabhai to come to the dais and introduced him to the congregation, 'Dear children, here is a scientist. What do sciences do? All of us experience, including this church, the light from electricity. I am able to talk to you through the mike which is made possible by science. The treatment of patients by doctors comes from medical sciences. Science through technology enhances the comfort and quality of human life. What do I do as a preacher? I pray for you, for your well-being, for your peace. In short, what Vikram is doing and what I am doing is: working for well-being of human beings in an integrated way, materially and spiritually. Dear children, Vikram Sarabhai says that he would build within a year alternative facilities for us near the sea coast. Now dear children, can we give our abode, and can we give God's abode, for a great scientific mission?' There was total silence, a pin-drop silence. Then all of them got up and said Amen together. Their unified voice made the church building reverberate. This church thus became the starting point for many space-related scientific and technological activities.

Later, the Thumba Equatorial Rocket Launching Station (TERLS) led to the establishment of the Vikram Sarabhai Space Centre (VSSC) and multiple space centres throughout the country. Today, the church has become an important centre of learning, where thousands of people learn about the dynamic history of the space programme of India and the great minds of a scientist and a spiritual leader. Of course, the citizens of Thumba got well-equipped facilities, a worshiping place and an educational centre at another place at the right time. When I think of this event, I can see how enlightened spiritual and scientific leaders can converge towards giving reverence to human life.

Now let us discuss the third important component of enlightened society, which is the achievement of economic development for societal transformation.

Economic Development for Societal Transformation

The Indian economy is in an ascending phase. There is considerable growth in the manufacturing and service sectors. We have a mission of spreading this economic growth throughout the country, including the rural sector. Nearly 220 million people in both rural and urban areas have to be uplifted by upgrading their quality of life. Even though the GDP indicates our economic growth, people's participation is essential for achieving the required targets. It is essential to ensure that the citizens have a good quality of life, encompassing nutritious food, good habitat, clean environment, affordable healthcare, quality education and productive employment. In other words, we propose to create a knowledge society.

KNOWLEDGE SOCIETY

Knowledge has always been the prime mover of prosperity. A knowledge society is one of the basic foundations of the development of any nation. Knowledge has many forms and it is available at many places. The acquisition of knowledge has been the thrust throughout the world, and sharing is a unique culture of our country. Economic growth for India is fundamentally tied to societal transformation in the knowledge products and services sector. This in turn strengthens agriculture and manufacturing through innovation and value addition. Our multi-dimensional movement towards Developed India 2020 aims to generate revenue not only from raw materials, agricultural and industrial products, which are the hallmarks of an agricultural society, but also through information and knowledge in the form of knowledge-intensive products and skills.

Knowledge Society and Creativity

In a knowledge society, we have to make innovations continuously. Innovations come through creativity. Creativity comes from beautiful minds. It can happen anywhere and in any part of the world. It may start from a fisherman's hamlet or a farmer's household or a dairy farm or cattle breeding centre, or it could emanate from classrooms or labs or industries or R&D centres. Creativity has got multiple dimensions such as inventions, discoveries and innovations. The creative mind has the ability to imagine or invent something new by combining, changing or reapplying existing ideas. The creative person is open to change and newness, is willing to play with ideas and possibilities, has flexibility of outlook, and enjoys what is good, while looking for ways to improve it. Creativity is a process through which we can continuously improve ideas and find unique solutions by making gradual alterations and refinements to our works. The important aspect of creativity is: seeing the same thing as everybody else, but thinking of something different.

Dimensions of Knowledge Society

In the knowledge economy, the objective of a society changes from fulfilling the basic needs of all-round development to empowerment. The education system will be promoted by creative, interactive, self-learning formal and informal education with focus on values, merit and quality. The workers, instead of being skilled or semi-skilled, will be knowledgeable, self-empowered and flexibly skilled. The type of work, instead of being structured and hardware driven, will be less structured and software driven. The management style will emphasize more on delegation rather than giving command. Impact on environment and ecology will be strikingly less compared to industrial economy. Finally, the economy will mostly be driven by knowledge and knowledge-driven industry.

Using the knowledge society as a base, we have to realize societal transformation by creating 7,000 PURA (Providing Urban Amenities in Rural Areas) covering 600,000 villages in different parts of India.

PURA Mission

PURA envisages economic empowerment of a cluster of villages through the provision of physical connectivity, electronic connectivity and knowledge connectivity leading to economic connectivity. Based on the terrain and climatic conditions, there could be four types of PURA in our country—plain terrain, hill, coastal and desert. The population in the plain terrain and coastal region PURA may be around 20,000 to 100,000 in a cluster of 20 to 30 villages, whereas in the hill or desert PURA, the population may be 7,500 to 15,000 in a cluster of 30 to 50 villages.

Typical Working PURAs

It is possible to get an insight of PURA by studying a few of the operational PURAs in different parts of the country, in Periyar, Loni, Chitrakoot and Byrraju. Let us highlight some of the operational PURAs.

Periyar PURA (Tamil Nadu): The Periyar PURA complex, pioneered by the Periyar Maniammai College of Technology for Women, Vallam, Tanjore, is functioning near Vallam in a cluster of over 65 villages with a population of 1 lakh. This PURA complex has all the three connectivities—physical, electronic and knowledge—leading to economic connectivity. The centre of activity emanates from the women's engineering college that provides the electronic and knowledge connectivity. Periyar PURA has healthcare centres, primary- to postgraduate-level education and vocational training centres. This has resulted in large-scale employment generation and creation of a number of entrepreneurs with the active support of 850 self-help groups. Two hundred acres of wasteland has been transformed into cultivable land with innovative water management schemes such as contour ponds and water sheds for storing and irrigating the fields. The villagers plant jatropha, herbal and medicinal plants, generate power using bio-mass, process food and run marketing centres. This model has emanated independent of any government initiative. A committed leadership has been provided by the engineering institution. Recently, five of Periyar PURA villages were connected through Wi-MAX Wireless, having minimum 4 mbps connectivity, with the Periyar PURA nodal centre. This connectivity provides sustainable economic development in that region.

One Village One Product and PURA: The members of Periyar PURA have entered into a strategic partnership with Japan External Trade Organization (JETRO) of Japan. During the last eight months, the people of Periyar PURA villages, technologically supported by Periyar Maniammai College of Engineering for Women, have worked with experts from JETRO on various products for which core competence and raw material is available in Thanjavur district. They developed prototypes for products such as bed sheets, table runners, cushion covers, brass drums, curtains, bread baskets etc. Interaction with JETRO specialists included comparison with Japanese products, discussion on raw material selection, technical advice on product development and final quality inspection. Based on this intensive interaction, the villagers produced 123 products and JETRO selected forty out of them for the international market. These products were exhibited in Delhi and Tokyo and they attracted the interest of hundreds of visitors.

Loni PURA (Maharashtra): In Loni PURA in Maharashtra, a participative model of integrated rural development has come up among forty-four villages with a population of 80,000 people. The Loni PURA model has been pioneered by the Pravara Medical trust. It is improving the productivity of the rural people through improved quality of life with healthcare, education and employment. The concept is people-centric development for social transformation. The thrust of development has been on comprehensive medical care, particularly for women and children, need-based health education and e-connectivity to the farmers. The complex has created twenty-seven educational and vocational institutions consisting of schools, colleges, and polytechnics, including medical and engineering colleges. It has also created a sugar factory, biogas and chemical plants and power projects. They have a large number of self-help groups for providing loans at low interest for the weaker sections of society. Due to the cooperative effort of the people, literacy in these villages has gone up from 63 per cent to 83 per cent, birth rate has come down, infant mortality rate has decreased to 35 per 1000 from 70 per 1000 and the standard of living has gone up by over 20 per cent compared to other villages in the neighbouring areas.

Byrraju PURA: Byrraju Foundation of Satyam near Bhimavaram has undertaken the mission of establishing 32 Ashwini centers benefiting 116 villages with a population of around 500,000 people. It has provided wireless (512 kbps to 2 mbps) electronic connectivity and knowledge connectivity in cooperation with National Academy of Construction, Hyderabad and other domain experts, thereby creating economic connectivity in these villages. During the last four years of its operation, it has developed skill and knowledge in areas such as construction, tailoring, garment production, IT and spoken English. This resulted in 3000 jobs with a minimum earning of Rs 3000 per month, which is three times that of their earlier earning potential. A rural BPO Gram IT, established in Jallikakinada centre, has trained unemployed graduates in IT skills and spoken English, and employed hundred people in BPO operations such as back office processing of human resource data of Satyam Computers; and data processing of one million self-help group members of Andhra Pradesh under the programme of 'Mapping the bottom of the Pyramid'.

This Gram IT BPO has effected a 10 per cent reverse migration from Hyderabad to Bhimavaram. This model can be replicated by many of our IT companies in the rural sector to create PURA clusters and bring rural transformation. For realizing economic prosperity equitably, we need to build the ethics of the nation. Clean environment, healthy lifestyle, people empowered with education with a value system, religion transforming into spirituality and economic development with inclusive growth are the pre-requisites for the birth of a noble nation.

PROMOTING PEACEFUL AND PROSPEROUS SOCIETY

Philosopher-President of India S. Radhakrishnan compared the knowledge centres of various civilizations. The Delphi

Temple says *know thyself* just as the Upanishads say *atmanam viddhi*. He also stated that the greatest of civilizations 'does not depend upon the extent of territory which they have or the size of the population which they embrace, but it depends upon the artistic, intellectual and spiritual achievements of the countries themselves.'

The development that took place during the twentieth century had improved the condition of human life but conflicts in our day-to-day life remained. A peaceful and prosperous society remains elusive. How do we realize such a society? One of the important components of a noble nation is paving the way for unity of minds in a diverse world. Certain experiences in our own country and elsewhere reveal that unity of minds is possible. On this subject of unity of minds, there were discussions between Acharya Mahapragya and me on different occasions.

Pilgrimage for World Peace

Acharya: I took the spiritual path. You structured your own life. How do you describe your experience?

Kalam: Strength and dignity come out of struggle. I would like to recall my travel in Durban, South Africa, on 16 September 2004. The train halted at Pietermartizburg, the station where the monster of apartheid bit Gandhiji on the cold winter night of 7 June 1893. He was evicted out of a first class compartment because of the colour of his skin.

Acharya: This was the rebirth of Ahimsa Dharma after the Kalinga War in 300 BC.

Kalam: Fortunately there is continuity, Acharyaji. You are promoting the principle of non-violence in a mission mode. When I was standing at Pietermartizburg railway station, two scenes were fresh in my mind. One was of

Robben Island where Nelson Mandela had been imprisoned for twenty-six years in a very small cell, and the other scene was that of his house.

Acharya: Tell me what you felt when you were in Robben Island?

Kalam: In Robben Island the freedom of individuals was chained. I met Ahmed Kathrada there who was a co-prisoner with Nelson Mandela. What surprised me was the smallness of the room where the six-foot tall Nelson Mandela was kept for twenty-six years. He used to be taken for quarrying to the nearby mountain under the harsh sun, which damaged his eyesight. In spite of sustained torture, he revealed to the world his indomitable spirit. It is during this time that he evolved a manuscript of freedom in tiny letters every day, when the jail wardens went to sleep. This small tiny-lettered manuscript finally became the famous book of Mandela, *A Long Walk to Freedom*.

Acharya: What was the other event?

Kalam: When I entered Nelson Mandela's house, his cheerfulness struck me. When I was leaving his house, he came to the portico to give me a send-off, and as he walked he discarded his walking stick and made me his support. While walking, I asked him, 'Dr Mandela, can you please tell me about the pioneers of the anti-apartheid movement in South Africa?' He responded spontaneously, 'Of course. One of the greatest pioneers of South Africa's anti-apartheid movement was M.K. Gandhi. India gave us M.K. Gandhi, and we gave you back Mahatma Gandhi after two decades. Mahatma Gandhi was an apostle of non-violence.'

Acharya: M.K. Gandhi arrived in South Africa and returned to India as Mahatma Gandhi! It is indeed a beautiful and true statement by Nelson Mandela. Could you tell me, what is unique about Nelson Mandela?

Kalam: When Nelson Mandela became the President of South Africa, he gave those who had indulged in apartheid and had ill-treated and put him in the jail for twenty-six years, the freedom to move and live in South Africa as equal citizens. The greatness of the spirit shown by Nelson Mandela is beautifully captured by the poet Thiruvalluvar:

இன்னா செய்தாரை ஒறுத்தல் அவர்நாண
நன்னயம் செய்து விடல்

'For those who do ill to you, the best punishment is to return good to them.' This characteristic among leaders is essential for promoting harmony and peace in society.

Acharya: Do you have a similar experience in India?

Kalam: During my peace pilgrimage, I visited Apapuri in Bihar—the sinless town. There is a beautiful temple of white marble where Lord Mahavira had delivered his sermons. I went to Jal Mandir, the place where Lord Mahavira attained Nirvana. I saw lotus flowers around me blooming in the lake, and remembered another couplet of Thiruvalluvar:

வெள்ளத் தனைய மலர்நீட்டம மாந்தர்தம்
உள்ளத் தனைய துயர்வு

'Whatever be the depth or the state of cleanliness of the pond, the lotus flower springs out and blooms majestically looking towards the sun.' Similarly, human life can be transformed into purposeful high living only when a great aim engulfs the mind of the individual.

Acharya: You are blessed. What message did you get there?

Kalam: I am humbled to share with you. Lord Mahavira taught that human beings derive their own salvation and that is through three jewels: Right Faith, Right Knowledge and Right Conduct.

Mahavira rejected the demarcations of the caste system and raised his voice against all forms of intolerance and discrimination. He also resisted and rejected efficiency of rituals devoid of purity of thoughts, words and deeds. I could see a convergence between knowledge as power and knowledge for salvation.

Acharya: Jain philosophy and ethics are virtually synonymous with the principles of ahimsa, which run through the Jain tradition like a golden thread. Ahimsa enjoys a singular centrality in the Jain faith. What else did you capture in Bihar?

Kalam: Bihar is a blessed land. I visited the Bihar School of Yoga at Munger, which guides yoga projects and medical research associations with prestigious hospitals drawing inspiration from Adi Sankaracharya. I visited Khanquah Rahmani, a holy shrine established over hundred years ago by the eminent Sufi Hazrat Moulana Mohammed Ali. During the discussions that I had with some young people at the shrine, I shared one of the messages of the Prophet:

When you speak, speak the truth.
Perform what you promise.
Discharge your trust.
Withhold your hand from striking and taking,
That which is unlawful and bad.

Acharya: Let us follow this path and lead a noble life. Of course, you would have visited Bodh Gaya.

Kalam: I went to the Maha Bodhi temple where Lord Buddha got enlightenment. I visited Takht Shri Harmandir Sahib in Patna, which is the birthplace of Shri Guru Gobind Singh. In all these places, I found that great souls had propagated the philosophy of good life, and above all, these centres provided a harmonious multi-religious environment for the people to live in peace and happiness. When I visited all these places of importance, I felt that Bihar is the right place to start Unity of Minds.

Acharya: Kalam, you indeed had a pilgrimage. I heard in your lectures about your Tawang experience. Let us discuss that.

Kalam: Indeed I had two great experiences. During the year 2003, I visited a Buddhist monastry at Tawang in Arunanchal Pradesh. I was asking myself what is the unique feature of Tawang and the surrounding villages that makes the people and monks so much at peace with themselves. When the time came, I asked the chief monk the reason behind the peace and happiness radiated by everyone. He said, 'In the present world, we have a problem of distrust and unhappiness transforming into violence.'

Acharya: The reverend monk was right in telling you this. When you remove 'I' and 'Me' from your mind, you will eliminate ego; if you get rid of ego, hatred towards fellow human beings vanishes; if the hatred goes out of our mind, violence in thinking and action disappears; if violence is taken away, peace springs in human minds. Then peace and only peace blossoms in the society.

Kalam: I realized the meaning of the beautiful equation for peaceful life. But it is a difficult mission for the individual to remove the ethos of 'I' and 'Me'.

Acharya: This has to come out of education—from childhood learning in schools and through association with great Acharyas. What was the second experience?

Kalam: I visited an ancient Christian monastery in RILA, located in the hills of Bulgaria. It is the biggest Bulgarian Revival spiritual and cultural centre with a 16,000-volume library, including 134 manuscripts from the fifteenth to the nineteenth century. This holy site played an important role in the spiritual and social life of medieval Bulgaria. Destroyed by fire at the beginning of the nineteenth century, the complex was rebuilt later and is now surrounded by a big fort. While in that divine environment, amidst the Reverend Fathers aged between eighty and ninety, I felt like praying. I went to the altar and asked permission of the Reverend Bishop to recite the part of the prayer of St. Francis of Assisi. The prayer was repeated by all the people present in the monastery.

Lord, make me an instrument of Your peace;
Where there is hatred let me sow love;
And where there is injury, pardon;
And where there is doubt, faith;
And where there is despair, hope;
And where there is darkness, light;
And where there is sadness, joy.
For it is in giving that we receive;
...it is in pardoning that we are pardoned;
...and it is in dying that we are born to eternal life.

Acharya: Kalam, your mind has been trained with beautiful events and spiritual thoughts. Let me pray for your success in the mission of promoting world peace. May this beautiful divine message of love enlighten your life.

ETHICS FOR THE NATION

So far we have discussed evolution of human life and evolution of human society. Birth of a noble nation would need studying the challenges faced by society due to the continuous process of growth and environmental deterioration and finding a sustainable solution to remedy the damage and promote a conflict-free society for posterity. This would require working for a clean, green environment, developing a healthy society through a three-pronged model and making enlightened citizens through value-based education, transforming religion into spirituality and above all creating a poverty- and illiteracy-free nation. Also, we have discussed the promotion of Unity of Minds among citizens for generating a happy society. All this can be realized if the entire nation has an ethos of 'work with integrity and succeed with integrity'. Where does it start? How can the national ethics be evolved? We propose the following algorithm.

A nation has to have ethics in all its tasks for sustained economic prosperity and peace.
If a nation is to have ethics, society has to promote ethics and value systems.
If society is to have ethics and value systems, families should adhere to ethics and value systems.
If families have to evolve with ethics and value systems, parenthood should have inbuilt ethics.
Parental ethics come from great learning, value-based education and creation of clean environment that leads to righteousness in the heart.

There is a beautiful connectivity between heart, character, nation and the world. In a society, we have to build righteousness among all its constituents. For society as a whole to be righteous, we need creation of righteousness in family, righteousness in education, righteousness in service, righteousness in career, righteousness in business and industry, righteousness in civil administration, righteousness in politics, righteousness in government, righteousness in law and order and righteousness in justice.

We conclude this book with a prayer for peace in the mind of every individual and the prosperity of the nation.

Where there is righteousness in the heart,
There is beauty in the character.
When there is beauty in the character,
There is harmony in the home.
When there is harmony in the home,
There is order in the nation.
When there is order in the nation,
There is peace in the world.

—A divine hymn

Postscript

Soul is my God,
Renunciation is my prayer,
Amity is my devotion,
Self-restraint is my strength,
Non-violence is my religion.

—Acharya Mahapragya

Our vision: People living in a clean, green environment, having prosperity without poverty, living in peace without fear of war, a happy place to live for all citizens of the nation.

—A.P.J. Abdul Kalam

The joint family system is not widely accepted as a justifiable field of study today because more and more individuals are opting for a nuclear family consisting of two parents and children. The content of popular television programmes and print media has also encouraged the trend of people moving away from the joint family system. The notion and application of an achievement-centric philosophy entrenched in materialistic consumption certainly reduces the significance of family values. Given the sizable number of young children growing up in our society without the guidance of experienced parents and grandparents, the consequences of this trend are far-reaching and will decide the very future of our nationhood.

We have discussed in the book the pluralistic nature of Indian society with multiple class and cultural traditions. Indian people have ingrained belief systems and values, driven by their cultural norms. In a multi-ethnic society, the cultural institutional structure embraces kinship, education, religion, property and economy, recreation, and certain modalities. The reality of contemporary India is its plural society lacking a common value system. Under these seemingly conflicting and unstable conditions, order and control functions become a premium.

Clearly, cultural coexistence under the traditional pluralist model had bred ethnic cleavage and closure, with only minimal participation of the rural population in the growing economy. Also, there has been sub-optimal social interaction between various religious groups. However, ethnic cleavage and closure has become diluted since competing ethnic groups have begun to perceive themselves as holding a similar class position at each level in the class structure. Indeed, the possibility still exists for people of similar ethnicity and race, but from different class levels to experience prejudice and discrimination. Any of the three factors of class, and ethnicity, or their combination is capable of triggering off prejudice and discrimination and undo the hard work of economic development. A noble nation essentially transcends all forms of inequality.

How to break the cycle of perpetual inequality in Indian society? Though each group's culture is distinctive, yet it is permeable. By making righteousness as an axis, the integrated pluralist paradigm of living in harmony can be created. This integrated pluralist model will have the potential to facilitate a focus on ethnic similarities and not ethnic differences, thereby preserving the aspirations of multiple groups in a dominant culture.

A false assumption is sometimes used to promote assimilation into a common Indian culture, as the focus is kept mainly on ethnic differences. The false assumption is that inequality can be resolved by creating a common culture, achieved only through assimilation. A spotlight on ethnic similarities will preserve and advance each other's culture. Picture the bridge of righteous living and the coalitions based on non-violence and peaceful coexistence as cultural universals underlying our subcultures. Whole cultures cannot be bridged and should not be bridged. It should be sufficient to connect components common to different cultures. Joint families can be a cultural universal, for example.

The unit of the Indian village community has not been the individual but the joint family. A very important feature of this social unit has been that all property was held in common. The joint family system and kinship pattern could not be effectively relocated to the cities from villages, and it affected continuity between cultures, which was significant in enabling the family to socialize the child in the formative years.

The book calls for the first allegiance of an individual to his or her conscience, then to his or her family, next to the wider circle of kin, the community, and the society. A life based on righteousness and primarily around the family, and secondarily encompassing social and public life, is the hallmark of a great nation. The family-centred approach promotes particularistic values, and strong ethnic identification as attachment to family, village, state, and religion. This attachment, however, gets transformed into primary tasks for the individual, and encourages national politics. Many young Indian leaders, notwithstanding their localized psychological attachment, are using their ethnic base to integrate ethnicity and class into political activism while advancing to higher levels of cultural pluralism. In a period of economic weakness, ethnic cleavage and ethnic apportionment of blame can easily return us to servitude and poverty. We must never allow this to happen. We must start a process of mutual accommodation of each group's cultural values and increased informal interaction.

But who will do that?

We have thought over the question as to how a noble nation can be formed and have come to the conclusion that its seeds can be sown in a family. Only a good individual who has been brought up in the environment of a good family is able to realize his or her responsibility towards the nation. Such a citizen will adopt the principle 'work with integrity and succeed with integrity'.

Hence, we believe that it is possible to evolve a noble nation with the basic foundation of righteousness in the heart. Our people can live in a clean, green environment without pollution, prosper without poverty, experience peace without fear of war and have a happy place to live their lives. Thereby, our nation can become a model state for the evolution of noble society on the planet.

It is hoped that this book will be read with a feeling of deep understanding to explore how creation of a beautiful family will lead to the evolution of a noble nation.

Notes

CHAPTER 1

1. Tirthankar is one who by adopting asceticism achieves enlightenment (perfect knowledge), thus becoming a Jina (one who has conquered his inner enemies—anger, pride, deceit, desire etc.). A Tirthankar shows the path to enlightenment to others. The first Tirthankar was Rishabh. The twenty-fourth and last Tirthankar was Mahavir (599–527 BC).
2. The *Aitareya Upanishad* is one of the oldest of the Upanishads. It belongs to the Aitareya Aranyaka of the *Rigveda*. Divided into three chapters, it deals with the process of creation. The most famous expression of the Vedanta, 'pragnanarn Brahma,' which means Brahma is intelligence, comes from *Aitareya Upanishad*.
3. The *Chhandogya Upanishad* is one of the most prominent of philosophical and mystical texts. Among the ten major Upanishads, the *Chhandogya* and the *Brihadaranyaka* stand above others in their grand stature and majesty. The *Chandogya Upanishad* primarily deals with the visible forms of experience.
4. Mahayana (literally great vehicle) is one of the major branches of Buddhism. In the way of the Mahayana, enlightened wisdom is the main focus of realization. Compassion is gained through the transferral of merit and salvation, supported by a rich cosmography, including celestial realms and powers, with a spectrum of Bodhisattvas, both human and seemingly godlike, who can assist followers.

5. Purana is a corpus of Sanskrit legends and ancient Aryan beliefs. There are a total of eighteen major Puranas, all written largely in verse. These are divided into three groups, each exalting one member of the Hindu Trinity. The Puranas in which 'rajas' or passion prevails relate chiefly to Brahma (Brahma Purana, Brahmanda Purana, Brahmavayvarta Purana, Markandeya Purana, Bhavishya Purana, and Vamana Purana). The Puranas in which 'satva' or purity is the leitmotif is related to Vishnu (Vishnu Purana, Bhagavata Purana, Naradiya Purana, Garuda Purana, Padma Purana and Varaha Purana). Those in which 'tamas' or gloom and ignorance are dominant are related to Shiva (Shiva Purana, Linga Purana, Skanda Purana, Agni Purana, Matsya Purana, and Kurma Purana). Of the eighteen major Puranas, the Vishnu Purana is the most complete.
6. Acharya Tulsi (1914–1997) took his monk's vows at the age of eleven, and by the time he was sixteen, he had already started attracting acolytes. Acharya Kalugani (1909–1936) appointed him the Terapanth's ninth Acharya when he was just twenty-two. He started his Anuvrat Movement in 1952. He was against sectarianism and a proponent of Jain unity. Acharya Tulsi led many nationwide padyatras, logging over 100,000 km.
7. Thomas Stearns Eliot (1888–1965) was an American-born poet, dramatist, and literary critic, whose works, *The Waste Land* and *Four Quartets,* are considered major achievements of twentieth century Modernist poetry. Eliot wrote about people's ambitions being restricted by the mundane, repetitive nature of life and the human condition in general. He saw people living lives of survival, rather than enjoyment, in the new industrial age.

CHAPTER 2

1. Holy Quran 16.3; Sura *An-Nahl* (The Bee); *'Khalaqa assamawati walarda bilhaqqi taAAala AAamma yushrikoon.'*
2. The parable of the ancient city is given in the *Lankavatara Sutra*, one of the most important *sutras* (sacred texts) of Mahayana Buddhism. The cornerstone of the Chinese Chan and its Japanese version, Zen, the most important doctrine

given here is that of the primacy of consciousness, often called simply 'Mind Only', meaning that consciousness is the only reality. The sutra asserts that all the objects of the world, and the names and forms of experience, are merely manifestations of the mind.

3. Holy Quran 39.23; Sura *Az-Zumar*.
4. Psalm 1.13. Psalms is a book of the Hebrew Bible or *Tanakh*, and of the Old Testament of the Christian Bible. The Islamic redaction of the Book of Psalms is called the Zabur, and it is believed to be one of the holy books revealed by Allah prior to the Quran. The book is divided into 150 Psalms, each of which constitutes a religious song or chant. The first book comprises the first forty-one Psalms, all of which are ascribed to David.
5. Address by A.P.J. Abdul Kalam at the Human Rights Day function, 10 December 2002, at Vigyan Bhavan, New Delhi. All human beings are born free and equal in dignity and rights. They are endowed with reason and conscience and should act towards one another in a spirit of brotherhood. Everyone has the right to a standard of living adequate for the health and well-being of himself and of his family, including food, clothing, housing and medical care and necessary social services, and the right to security in the event of unemployment, sickness, disability, widowhood, or old age. All children, whether born in or out of wedlock, shall enjoy the same social protection.
6. Eusebius, *The History of the Church: from Christ to Constantine* (Penguin Classics, 1990).
7. Church of England, *Book of Common Prayer* (Oxford University Press, 2000).
8. Harold W. Percival, *Thinking and Destiny* (Motilal Banarasidass Publishers, 2001).

CHAPTER 3

1. Anaxagoras was a pre-Socratic Greek philosopher famous for introducing the cosmological concept of Nous (mind), the ordering force.

2. Eknath Easwaran, *The Dhammapada* (Nilgiri Press, New Edition, 1993).
3. Benedictus de Spinoza, *Spinoza: Complete Works* (Hackett Publishing Company, 2002).
4. G.W. Leibniz, *Philosophical Essays* (Hackett Publishing Company, 1989).
5. Arthur Schopenhauer, E.F.J. Payne (translator), *The World as Will and Representation* (Dover Publications, New Edition, 1966).
6. Alan W. Watts, *Behold the Spirit: A Study in the Necessity of Mystical Religion* (Vintage, 1972).
7. Walpola Rahula, *What the Buddha Taught* (Grove Press, 1974).
8. D.R. Gordon and D.B. Suits, *Epicurus: His Continuing Influence and Contemporary Relevance* (RIT Gay Graphics Art Press, 2003).
9. H. Ansbacher and R.R. Ansbacher, *Individual Psychology of Alfred Adler* (Harper Perennial, 1964).
10. A.P.J. Abdul Kalam and Y.S. Rajan, *India 2020: A Vision for the New Millennium* (Penguin Books, 1998)
11. Holy Quran 3.103. Sura *Al-Imran* (The Family of Imran).
12. Mattien Ricard and Christian Schmidt, *Journey for Peace: His Holiness the 14th Dalai Lama* (Scalo Publishers, 2005).
13. Leela D'Souza, *The Sociology of Religion: A Historical Review* (Rawat Publication, 2005).
14. Leonard Swidler is a professor of Catholic thought and inter-religious dialogue at Temple University since 1966. He is the editor of the *Journal of Ecumenical Studies* and author of over fifty books.

CHAPTER 4

1. Hippocrates (460 BC–380 BC) was an ancient Greek physician, commonly regarded as one of the most outstanding figures of all time in medicine. He has been called 'the father of medicine.' All graduating doctors are required to take the Hippocratic Oath before starting to practice medicine.

2. The Doctrine of Karma is a direct outcome of the extension of the age-old and well-established principle, 'as you sow, so you reap', to the spiritual sphere. In other words, this doctrine is nothing but an extension of the physical phenomenon observed in everyday experience in Nature that every action has a reaction, every effect has a cause, and vice versa. According to the Karma doctrine, the course of life of every living being here and hereafter is determined by his Karma or his deeds and a pious life leads to comforts, contentment and general well-being in the present life and re-birth in higher and better forms of existence. Evil actions result in birth in lower forms of existence in future life and unhappiness or misery in the present existence. In short, the doctrine may be summarized as the 'theory of inevitable consequences of one's actions'.
3. Ayurveda (Sanskrit ayu—life; veda—knowledge of) or Ayurvedic medicine is a comprehensive system of medicine, more than 5,000 years old and based on a holistic approach rooted in Vedic culture. The Charaka and Sushruta Samhitas are compendiums of two traditions rather than texts authored by single authors. A third tradition is that of the Kashyapas. The Ayurvedic idea is that the organism adapts to the environment and its food, climate etc. This principle of adaptation is called satyma. Through introducing small amounts of a food or medicine, the organism can adapt to its environment and learn to resist it.
4. The UN Declaration on Principles of Tolerance, 1995.
5. Attention-deficit hyperactivity disorder (ADHD) is a psychiatric diagnosis that interprets divergent personality traits perceived to be distracting as symptoms of a mental disorder. Characteristics sometimes interpreted as symptoms include hyperfocus, hyperactivity, social anxiety, forgetfulness, mood shifts, and disobedience. ADHD is commonly diagnosed among children. When diagnosed in adults, it is regarded as adult attention-deficit disorder (AADD). It is believed that approximately 30 to 70 per cent of children diagnosed with ADHD retain the disorder as adults. Adults with ADD are generally thought to have been undiagnosed as children.

6. Yoga is liberation from the bondage of limited thought, the conceptual mind, fabrication, and artificiality. Yoga frees us from superficiality, hollowness, attachment to neurotic external sublimation/ compensation and brings us into our more primary state of conscious existence. Yoga leads us into reality through our association with truth, love, light and peace. Hatha yoga does this through awakening the creative and evolutionary energy (kundalini), utilizing six major activities, namely: (1) purification exercises for the body, psychic nerves, and mind (kriyas); (2) positions that purify the body/mind and also build up psychic heat, inner psychic strength, and activate dormant circuitry (asanas); (3) the activation of various energy locks that prevent the dissipation of spiritual energy and accelerate the inner activation and natural evolutionary energy flow (bandhas); (4) consciously establishing a working relationship with our core energy and the source of prana mainly through breath control exercises (pranayama); (5) utilizing asana, bandha, pranayama, and visualization (dharanas) all at the same time in order to activate and accelerate the kundalini evolutionary energy through the psychic nerves and chakra system (mudra); and (6) abiding and cultivating consciously the state where dualistic thinking ceases.
7. The immune system is the system of specialized cells and organs that protect an organism from outside biological influences. In a broad sense, almost every organ has a protective function (such as the skin). When the immune system is functioning properly, it protects the body against bacteria and viral infections, destroying cancer cells and foreign substances. If the immune system weakens, its ability to defend the body also weakens, allowing pathogens, including viruses that cause common colds and flu, to grow and flourish in the body.

CHAPTER 5

1. Instinct is a preformed behavioural pattern, often manifesting itself immediately from birth. Its arrangement is determined

hereditarily and is repeated according to modalities relatively adapted to a certain kind of object. Sigmund Freud wavered between characterizing instinct as an organic stimulus—a 'need' affecting the psychic apparatus—and as a psychic representative of such an organic need-stimulus. Freud said that there must be pleasurable tensions and unpleasurable relaxations of tensions as well.

2. Supine means lying on one's back with face up. The opposite of supine is to prostrate, which means lying face downwards, often as the result of some accident or illness. Supine is also the opposite of prone, which is applied to patients in bed lying on their stomachs. There is an ancient saying from the Vedas: 'Desire first arose in IT'—and the world came into being, the divine seed of a world-to-be had first to feel the pulsing flame of desire to manifest before it could assume material form. So with every last one of us: we have to experience the desire to grow, to evolve, otherwise we are supine. The gods know only too well that supine individuals will never make their mark in spiritual (or even in material) things.

3. Psychology does not necessarily refer to the brain or nervous system and can be framed purely in terms of phenomenological or information processing theories of the mind. In Buddhism, psychological being is defined as sensation (vedanaa); conception (sanjnaa); volition (samskara); and consciousness (vijnana). In medical science it refers to unique characteristics of a person, namely personality, thought, reason, memory, intelligence and emotion. Jain Dharma emphasizes the importance of integration of opposites (for example, masculine and feminine, thinking and feeling, science and spirituality).

4. Right view (samyag-darshana) is the first actual step on the spiritual path. Without it, our subsequent steps are bound to be missteps. In the Jaina Yoga tradition, fourteen stages of inner evolution are distinguished. The first five stages are of interest to the present consideration: (l) False Vision (mithya-drishti), which is the typical confused state of mind of the average person; (2) Taste for Right Vision (sasvadana-samyag-drishti), which is the state of occasional understanding with

long lapses into semiconsciousness (spiritual ignorance); (3) Right and False Vision (samyag-mithya-drishti), which is the state of initial understanding mixed with wrong views; and (4) Lack of Self-Restraint but Right Vision (avirata-samyag-drishti), which is the state in which the practitioner has correct understanding but still lacks self-discipline to follow through consistently.

5. A part of the human brain called the reptilian brain (because it has similar functions to those of reptiles) does most of the processing of human emotional responses. These responses mostly occur automatically, as in the case of the familiar flight-or-attack response triggered by threatening situations. Humans have evolved in such a way that a 'neural-hijacking' takes place that provides a quick answer to life's critical situations. In humans, the reptilian brain has links with the neocortex, which can accordingly exert some control over the largely automatic responses of the reptilian brain.
6. Consciousness is like an iceberg, 90 per cent of it is underwater, invisible to the eye. Most of our behaviour patterns, and the causes of those behaviours, are automatic. The reasons for their occurrence are below our conscious awareness (in the subconscious). Awakening is the process of bringing what is below the conscious level up into conscious awareness. There are great benefits to awakening. When you awaken from the sleep-like trance of automatic behaviours, you feel more alive, you have more options at every moment, and you can make new choices that enable you to live the life you prefer. You discover who you really are. You become free, and can create your life more deliberately. Healing and love pour into your life and your relationships. Life becomes a joy instead of a struggle.
7. Stephen S. Covey, *The Seven Habits of Highly Effective People* (New York: Simon and Schuster, 1989).

CHAPTER 6

1. O.R. Krishnaswami, *The Wisdom of Thirukkural: A Guide to Living Commentary* (Bharatiya Vidya Bhavan, 2004).

2. Acharya Mahapragya and Nathamal, *Jainism: Ethics and Morality* (Anmol Publications, 2000).
3. Howard Gardner, *Five Minds for the Future* (Harvard Business School Press, 2007).

Index

About the Authors

ACHARYA MAHAPRAGYA is one of the most celebrated Jain thinkers of the world and is the tenth Acharya of the Jain Shwetambar Terapanth sect. Born in 1920 in Tamkor village in the Jhunjhunu district of Rajasthan, he became a monk at the age of ten. He got his education under the guidance of Acharya Shri Tulsi, who launched the Anuvrat Movement in 1949 to rid the world of violence and hatred and free religion from sectarianism.

A multidimensional personality and a renowned expert on Indian and Western philosophy and religion, Acharya Mahapragya is an erudite scholar of Jain Agamas and a coordinator of science and spiritualism. A prolific writer, he has been called a 'modern Vivekananda'. He has traversed more than 100,000 kilometres on foot and visited 10,000 villages to spread the message of nonviolence. To this purpose he embarked on an Ahimsa Yatra in 2001. He was honoured with the Communal Harmony Award in 2004 for his contribution in this field.

AVUL PAKIR JAINULABDEEN ABDUL KALAM was the President of India from 2002 to 2007, and is the recipient of the nation's highest civilian award, the Bharat Ratna. Born in 1931 in Rameshwaram in Tamil Nadu, Dr Kalam studied aeronautical engineering at the Madras Institute of Technology. He played a key role in the development of

India's first satellite launch vehicle, the SLV-3, and in the building and operationalization of India's strategic missile systems.

As Chairman of Technology Information, Forecasting and Assessment Council (TIFAC), he led an initiative with the help of 500 experts to arrive at Technology Vision 2020, giving a road map for transforming India into a developed nation. Dr Kalam has served as the Principal Scientific Advisor to the Government of India in the rank of Cabinet Minister, from November 1999 to November 2001, and was responsible for evolving policies, strategies and missions for many development applications.

As an elder statesman, he remains in the public eye for his role in offering counsel, reaching out to people and building bridges across religious and social divides. Dr Kalam's focus stays on transforming India into a developed nation by 2020 and to this end he has met and enthused three million youth.

The course of six LECTURES delivered by me in 1922 on Nadir Shah in India has been here compressed and re-arranged in three CHAPTERS. The reduction amounts to about one-sixth of the whole, but no essential fact or statement has been omitted.

J. Sarkar

Sir Jadunath Sarkar, CIE, FRAS (10 December 1870 – 19 May 1958) was a prominent Indian historian and a specialist on the Mughal dynasty. Sarkar was educated in English literature, worked as a teacher for some period of time but later shifted his focus to history research writing. He had vast knowledge of Persian language and all his books he wrote in English.